LEADERSHIP
FROM BEHIND
THE SCENES

LEADERSHIP
FROM BEHIND
THE SCENES

DR. RON WEBB

Acclaim Press
MORLEY, MISSOURI

Acclaim Press
— *Your Next Great Book* —

P.O. Box 238
Morley, MO 63767
(573) 472-9800
www.acclaimpress.com

Book Design: Devon Burroughs
Cover Design: M. Frene Melton

Library of Congress Control Number: 2015901149
ISBN-13: 978-1-938905-94-0
ISBN-10: 1-938905-94-6

First Printing: 2015
Printed in the United States of America
10 9 8 7 6 5 4 3 2 1

This publication was produced using available information.
The publisher regrets it cannot assume responsibility for errors or omissions.

ACKNOWLEDGMENTS

I would like to thank those who assisted me in developing this book. This is the hardest part, because there are so many people to thank. First of all, I would like to thank my wife, Georgia, who has encouraged me in so many ways and helped me to stay focused. I will also like to thank my children, Ron Jr., Tony, and Jackie, and my two grandsons, Jerrell Jr. and Jaxson, the future leaders.

I would like to thank my editors, Jeanne, Jami, and Jackie. I would also like to acknowledge my father, the late Alfonse Webb, Jr., and my mother, June Marie Webb; they are very special parents. All my siblings, from the oldest to youngest. Thanks to Dr. Sandra Jackson, for pushing me and encouraging me to stay the course and for her ability to enhance my ideas. And a special thanks to my advisor, Dave Webb, for his wisdom and insight. Also, I truly appreciate the wise counsel of my legal team, Clinton Summers and Jasper Edmundson. Furthermore, where would I be without help from Curtis Worley, Clinton Summers, Jr., and Benny Robertson.

And finally, I would like to thank my publisher, Doug Sikes, and his talented staff for making the book you now hold a reality.

CONTENTS

The Four Lethal Spirits

PREFACE

I am pleased to lend my endorsement of this book, *Leadership from Behind the Scenes,* by Bishop Ron Webb, my beloved constituent in the ministry. Reading this will enlighten those of you who are looking forward to someday being pastors in the church of our Lord Jesus Christ. I also believe this book will lend encouragement to those who are presently overseeing the flocks of God. It will strengthen your hearts by showing that you're not alone in some of the things you may be experiencing as you shepherdize God's sheep. I commend Bishop Webb for allowing the Lord Jesus Christ to inspire him in the production of this book.

-Bishop James A. Johnson, D.D., MTh.

FOREWORD

There have been many who have called Bishop Ron Webb "a Pastor to Pastors." I believe that. Not only has he been a Pastor to me, I proudly considered him to be one of my best friends and brothers. He was raised with the integrity and honor of both of his parents and holds faithful to his community. Despite the challenges in his life, he has built a ministry that has not only brought thousands to Christ but teaches others to do so. In Mark 6:4 (NCV) "Jesus said to them. A prophet is honored everywhere except in his hometown and with his own people and in his own home." In this instance, Bishop Ron Webb has managed to pastor a thriving church and numerous outreaches throughout the community in which he was born and raised. He is highly respected by both his hometown and all over the World.

Bishop Webb has built a reputation for his God given wisdom, which makes him sought after by leaders from all over the country and asked to speak to their congregations and in pastor's conferences. For me, he is my main "go to" person for advice, which is why I nominated him myself for the Board of Directors here at Morningside. This is a man that has fulfilled every definition of friendship and loyalty; the kind of person you can call on day or night and you know he will answer with an unfailing heart. No matter what is happening in my life or in his, he always, ALWAYS has a word for me.

You can find out a lot about a person when working side by side with them as I did while helping to re-build a town devastated by the Mississippi River flood. There is a tendency to bond together when involved in mission work, and it can be both physically and emotionally exhausting. Throughout my friendship with him, I have never doubted his steadfast faith. But what was revealed to me in that cherished time was Bishop Ron Webb's heart to serve and love others.

Leadership from Behind the Scenes is an honest and bold look at the challenges of building a ministry in today's world. I believe that many do not understand the specialty that is involved in this type of work. We in ministry are passionate about following the Lord's will. We have a burning devotion to Christ and the incredible calling upon our spirit. There are a multitude of careers in this world, but few that require not only your intelligence, creativity and drive, but your very soul. Ministry requires all of that and more.

Leadership is the key in any venture, but a Church cannot stand with only a leader. This book will help you build the support team that is required. Bishop Webb takes you step by step behind closed doors to the heart of ministry, the challenges of creating a staff that you can depend on and the heart breaking reality that things will go wrong. He will take you from the wisdom of delegation to guidance on keeping your staff from becoming bitter and burned out. And he will give crucial advice on the ability to stand by the phrase, "Teamwork Makes the Dream Work."

I have been in ministry for over fifty years. What is rarely spoken of in the Christian community are the challenges to a Pastor personally from the attacks, judgment and actions of others. All of the great men and women in the Bible also dealt with these issues. All who devote their lives to following Christ will struggle with this as well. Where there is favor, there is also a fight and you will experience this in your ministry work. Bishop addresses topics such as the importance of humility, forgiveness and understanding. He encourages us to support one another and not compete in the body of Christ. He teaches us that there will be divine connections in our lives as well as demonic ones and how to spot the warning signs. And he will advise us on the necessity and process of confrontation; reminding us that the Bible is a book of confrontations and that it is your duty as a leader to confront issues to avoid a ministry that can and will fracture.

In my opinion, there is no finer man of integrity and wisdom as Bishop Ron Webb. Within these pages you will find years of service, compassion, leadership, dedication and understanding from the heart of the Pastor to Pastors. *Leadership from Behind the Scenes* is one of those tools of instruction that I feel God has brought to me and my Ministry, and I believe it is full of wisdom and advice that will benefit all Pastors and those in leadership roles; young or old, new or well-seasoned.

James 1:5 (NIV)

"If any of you lacks wisdom, you should ask God, who gives generously to all without finding fault, and it will be given to you."

Thank you God for Bishop Ron Webb and his continuing passion to serve You. Thank you for his leadership and guidance. Thank you for his unfailing call to follow Your Word, Wisdom and Compassion. Thank you Lord, for this man I call my friend.

-Jim Bakker

INTRODUCTION

Often we, as leaders, find ourselves wearied and battle-scarred along life's journey. Perhaps you will see yourself within these pages and relate on some level. In fact, you may be surprised how much we have in common. Thomas Edison once said that he failed his way to success. It's much the same with ministry. There are no perfect leaders and no flawless followers. Sometimes you will fail, and other times you will succeed. You can't be a leader without responsibility, making tough decisions, standing up for what is right, setting a good example, having a vision, and forgiving. Likewise, you will also be hurt, lied about, falsely accused, and wrongly judged. You will experience both victories and defeats. It all comes with the territory.

I often wonder why leaders are reluctant to be transparent with others. They refuse to acknowledge the struggles that come with ministry. We tend to show our successful side instead of the alternate view where we too have failures. Failures that sometimes delay or prevent victory all together. In this book, real and relevant issues are addressed such as the constant pressure to perform. This book is specifically designed for ministry leaders to help improve their outlook on life (e.g. for those depressed or anxious) and relationships or interactions with others (e.g. for those with difficulty managing anger, communicating needs or tolerating stress). We take our "rock star" persona on stage with us, while *Behind the Scenes* we are increasingly fearful leaders, frustrated pastors, bitter children, and depressed pastor's wives. I'm reminded of a time when I went to an upscale restaurant that served excellent food and gave impeccable service, and the ambiance was extraordinary. After enjoying a fantastic meal, I excused myself to use the restroom. However, I accidently wandered into a back area, and I recall thinking it was a war zone. Obscenities were being hurled, voices were elevated, and items tossed. I stood in silence and observed how the waiters and hostesses moved from chaos to calm in a matter of minutes as they transitioned from the back to the dining area. I thought, *Wow, isn't that the picture of ministry.* At the surface level all seems well, but it's another story when you go *Behind the Scenes.*

Ministry comes with many challenges including, but not limited to, those of faith, finances, and family. One day you are full of faith and power, the next day fearful and weak. Ministry is messy! Proverbs 14:4 says, *"Where no oxen are, the crib is clean..."* We lead and feed, but we also bleed. We encourage others, but there are times we need encouragement. We pour into others, when we need replenishing. Often we help others, when we ourselves are hurting. If the truth be told, many times the counselor needs counseling and the doctor needs healing. In ministry, there will come a time when the leader will be required to take the same medicine that he has prescribed to others. Leaders are expected to be perfect, but newsflash...we are not perfect, but chosen. As a result, many hide behind a mask and play the role that ministry demands. Just like professional actors, we try hard to stay in character and desperately seek the accolades of critics. Truth be told, we are more like Clark Kent than Superman. The same grace and mercy that works for the people in the pew also extends to the pulpit.

I was inspired to write this book to provide guidance and easy to grasp information to assist leaders in ministry to avoid pitfalls and advance the kingdom. Today more than ever, pastors are not just leaving their pulpits, but the ministry altogether. It's both alarming and tragic. In reality, many active leaders do not know or are not comfortable with discussing the challenges and complexities associated with ministry. Unfortunately, up until now, leaders have not had much guidance and have silently struggled. You'll also find tools and ideas presented in this book for destroying the illusion that the ministry and its leaders are perfect. This book is not about what your ministry does or doesn't do; that's your business. This book is about how to move forward in an authentic way. When we are courageous enough to go *Behind the Scenes,* we can learn that our true calling is to be faithful, not famous, and to always keep in mind that we are servants, not celebrities.

-Bishop Ron Webb

LEADERSHIP
FROM BEHIND
THE SCENES

CHAPTER 1

THE COST OF THE COAT

Not all of your persecutions will happen outside of the church. In fact, most of your attacks will come from within its walls. It's true; the people you love can hurt you like no one else can. They have the innate ability to rip your heart right out of your chest. But in order to grow you must also forgive. Perhaps the best example of this is depicted in the life of Joseph in the Bible. You can read about it in Genesis, chapter 37.

Joseph was a man anointed to dream, and his brothers hated him for it because of the content of that dream. Joseph's dream revealed that he would one day rule over his brothers, and they were not happy about it. In fact, the Word of God says in verse 18 that *they conspired against him to slay him.*

Don't let anyone kill your dream. Be cautious of those who would speak negative things over your dream, and ultimately destroy it. Keep on dreaming, and dream big.

As long as you are on the same level as those around you, all is well. But with promotion comes persecution. Remember, there will be no advancement without adversity, no conquering without conflict, no building without battling, and no opportunity without opposition. God will prepare you before He positions you. We are dealing with a generation of young leaders who want power, position, and prestige but don't want to go through the process. In order to get to it, you must first go through it. There is no success without struggle. There are only two jobs in the world that start on top, digging a well and digging a grave.

Now, all of us enjoy the favor of God in our lives. But much like Joseph and his coat of many colors, the people around you will become envious. Of course, the coat of favor looks inviting and important, but it will cost you to put it on. When the favor of God is on your life, it will attract enemies.

You may be wondering why there have been so many attacks on you. It's because the hand of God is on your life. Your anointing will draw the fire of the enemy. If you have experienced any level of success, you have become a target. Now all of your enemies will start shooting at you. But please do not take off the coat. Wear it in style and find a matching hat! Shake your finger in the enemy's face and tell him, "God favors me!"

Another example of favor can be found in the book of Ruth. While Ruth served her mother-in-law, Naomi, she had no idea that she was walking into a blessing. She was already working in her field of favor. Soon Ruth went from working in the field to owning the field. Stewardship precedes leadership.

In this season of your life, you will no longer have to search for favor. It will find you. You will see that by continuing to faithfully serve God, the favor will fall on you.

In the Name of Jesus, I decree and declare the favor of God over your life. Favor over your family, favor in your finances, and favor in every facet of your life. I prophesy favor over your church and your ministry. From this day forward, do not be ashamed of the favor of God on your life. Enjoy it. It is from God. Don't try to explain it; just proclaim it and speak it over your life every day.

The Price of Wearing the Coat

Because of the coat, there was a separation between Joseph and those he loved. The Bible says,

> *"And it came to pass, when Joseph was come unto his brethren, that they stripped Joseph out of his coat, his coat of many colors that was on him; and they took him, and cast him into a pit: and the pit was empty, there was no water in it.... Then there passed by Midianites merchant-men; and they drew and lifted up Joseph out of the pit, and sold Joseph to the Ishmaelite's for twenty pieces of silver: and they brought Joseph into Egypt."* Genesis 37:23-24, 28

All of this was in the will of God. Joseph ended up in the pit because of the coat, but that's where God began to develop something in him and through him.

Maybe you feel as if you are in the pit today, but every one of us ends up there at some point in our lives. Don't reject it; respect it.

Joseph had his pit just like Jesus had His Gethse-mane—which in name means *pressure* or *olive press*. Often we are pressed beyond measure. What God is doing in us will not happen in a moment. It is a process. If we can handle the process, the outcome will be great in power. Joseph was left feeling crushed, but it was all in God's plan. Behind the process of crushing there is something being produced in our lives. Crushed grain produces fine flour, crushed grapes produce fine wine, crushed olives produce the anointing oil, and crushed rose petals produce fine fragrances—hence the thorn before the rose. So if you endure the process, you will enjoy the promise. Remember, there is a cost to this coat!

It Happened in the House

As we continue to look at the life of Joseph, we find him in Genesis, chapter 39 being sold into Potiphar's cabinet. The tables were turning for him. He could finally see some light at the end of his tunnel.

Have you ever been there? You feel like things are finally getting better, only to realize that they are actually getting worse?

Now we see Joseph being promoted. You can't keep a good man down! The steps of a good man are ordered by the Lord. God not only orders our steps, but He also orders our stops. God's hand was upon Joseph's life, and everything he touched prospered. The Bible says in verse 5 that the Lord blessed the Egyptian's house for Joseph's sake. It's called being blessed by association. Wherever you are placed or positioned, if God's hand is on you, no one can set his or her hand against you. Watch your connections, and be aware of who you come into covenant with.

The Word of God says, *"If God be for us, who can be against us?"* Romans 8:31

Just as things are looking up for Joseph, an attack comes in the form of Potiphar's wife. The Bible tells us that Joseph was fair to look upon. So when Sister Potiphar walked by and saw him working, she found him tempting. She opened the door and gave him an invitation, but he wasn't interested. The bedroom was calling, but Joseph was hauling!

So now we find Joseph being falsely accused and it seems like the dream is not panning out. Instead of the sun, moon, and stars bowing to him, it looks as if he is bowing to them. Joseph knows in his heart that he is the head, but it looks like he is the tail. He is really above, though it seems he is beneath. He will be the lender, but it appears as though he is the borrower. We fight unseen forces on a daily basis. Principalities and powers constantly war against us. In the life of the believer spiritual warfare never ceases; it is a fight every single day. Sometimes our destiny is in disguise. We know where we need to go, but we're not always sure how to get there.

At this point, Joseph was made to look guilty when he was actually innocent. Many doors open, but not every good door is a God door. Joseph may have lost his coat, but he kept his character.

What do you do when you know in your heart that you are innocent, but all the evidence points to the contrary? We think that pressure only builds character, but pressure will *reveal* character.

Joseph went to prison for something he did not do. However, while in prison, he still dreamed. It's interesting to note that his gift was still at work in prison. Joseph interpreted the dream of both the butler and the baker. He prophesied that the butler would be restored to his rightful place. He asked in return that the butler remember him after he was restored.

What happens when those you've helped forget you? What happens when you have been there for them, but no one is there for you?

Joseph once again was left feeling very alone. As you may already know, many lonely days follow those in leadership.

Once again, the tides changed as Pharaoh had a dream that no one could interpret. Joseph was called on to interpret the dream and had a revelation of the time. Because of his interpretation, he was granted elevation.

Your gift will make room for you. Some things God designs that only you can do. Remain faithful in your calling. You never know when your next promotion is coming. Joseph went from a prisoner to being in charge, living large, high balling, and shot calling!

Things were now going great for Joseph. He's back on top. And then the same brothers that sold him out came to where he was. Joseph's heart was broken. He couldn't enjoy living in the palace because of the pain in his father's house. His pain did not come from outside his family; it happened inside his family.

Many of your attacks and much of your opposition will come from inside the house. For many of you reading this, your greatest hurt has come from the church. But you can't let that hinder you. Your fight is not for your past; the fight is for your future. It's not where you have been that makes hell nervous, but where you're going. Stop giving so much of your time to your past. Stop nursing it, cursing it, and rehearsing it. Turn around and reverse it! Say to the devil, *that was then, this is now.*

"And we know that all things work together for good to them that love God, to them who are the called according to His purpose." Romans 8:28

God designed everything that happened to Joseph—the good, the bad, and the ugly. You have to trust God even when you can't track him. He's working something behind the scenes. Joseph was now at the point in his life where he saw that everything he went through had to happen. It has often been said that if Joseph would have kept his mouth shut, he wouldn't have gotten into trouble. However, he had to share the dream in order to reach the place God had ordained.

Had he not shared the dream, his brothers would not have hated him.

Had they not hated him, he wouldn't have ended up in the pit.

Had he not been in the pit, he would not have been sold to Potiphar's cabinet.

Had he not been sold into slavery, he wouldn't have had the encounter with Potiphar's wife.

Had she not lied about him, he would not have gone to prison.

Had he not gone to prison, he wouldn't have interpreted Pharaoh's dream.

Had he not interpreted the dream, he wouldn't have been made Prime Minister, second only to Pharaoh. We see in the Bible where Joseph realized this.

"And Joseph said unto them, Fear not: for am I in the place of God? But as for you, ye thought evil against me; but God meant it unto good, to bring to pass, as it is this day, to save much people alive." Genesis 50:19-20

Remember, God will always prepare you before he positions you. Joseph says to his brothers, "Yes, you sold me, but God sent me." Joseph was able to have a relationship with his brothers again because he sought reconciliation instead of retaliation. Forgiveness is important. You have to forgive the people who have hurt or harmed you. Revenge in not your right. God tells us in Romans 12:19,

"Vengeance is mine; I will repay…"

The Gift of Manasseh

Joseph was thirty years old when he became Prime Minister of Egypt thirteen years after he was sold into slavery. With his position, he was given a wife, and to this union two sons were born. The first born he named Manasseh, meaning "to forget."

Joseph says in Genesis 41:51,

"For God, said he, hath made me forget all my toil, and all my father's house."

Wow. What a marvelous depiction of God's sovereign plan! In the midst of the things that are unfair and unjust, God's blessing will cause you to forget your past hurts.

Isaiah 61:3 says,

"To give unto them beauty for ashes, the oil of joy for mourning, the garment of praise for the spirit of heaviness…"

Joseph was given Manasseh as a sign of healing to replace his pain and hurt. Whatever you are going through, whoever has hurt you, God is able to heal you. Joseph could have wallowed in his pain or held on to his hurt, but instead God gave him a son and caused him to forget.

I encourage you to forgive the people who have hurt you and left you wounded or scarred. Remember, there is a Manasseh waiting for you! It will be as if it never happened. The rest of your life will be the best of your life.

When Joseph finally revealed himself to his brothers, God's blessings had already replaced his hurt.

He says in Genesis 45:5, 8,

"Now therefore, be not grieved, nor angry with your-selves, that ye sold me hither: for God did send me before you to preserve life...So now it was not you that sent me hither, but God..."

Just because God has released you from your hurt, it doesn't mean that it is permanently erased from your mind. Negative thoughts and despair will come. But the blessings of Christ outweigh the pain of human injustice and hopelessness in life. The blessings far outweigh the feelings of rejection, betrayal, and the guilt of past sins.

In conclusion, remember that God has a Manasseh blessing for you today! Accept His forgiveness and forgive those who've hurt you. Let God bring restoration to your life. You'll be glad you did.

Chapter 2

BALANCING THE LOAD

N ow let's take a look at the life of Moses. The name Moses means "to be drawn out." In Moses's day—just as in Jesus's day—a decree had been issued to kill every male child. The devil was fighting him before he was even born.

Anytime a death warrant is issued before your birth, you must be a threat to the kingdom of hell. The enemy wants to stop you before you even get started. He wants to abort your ambitions, block your blessings, jinx your joy, prevent your progress, hinder your hopes, and render you helpless. He only fights what he fears.

The enemy planned to kill Moses, but God used the enemy's plan to elevate him. Instead of being killed, Moses became a mighty deliverer for the children of Israel and led them out of Egypt.

In the wilderness Moses found himself carrying an incredible load. Ministry can become very weighty when you are engaged in battle after battle. We see in Exodus Chapter 17 where Israel was engaged in battle with Amalek. While Moses held his rod above his head, Israel prevailed. If he let down his arms, Israel started to lose. And as the battle grew longer, Moses began to weaken. Had not Aaron and Hur stepped in and held Moses's arms up for him, Israel would have lost the battle.

The same goes for ministry. If you are going to win, you have to have the right people working under you. Unity multiplies strength.

Henry Ford had it right when he said, "You can take my factories and burn up my buildings, but give me my people, and I will bring back my business every time."

The Importance of a Support Team

Every ministry has to have a good support team in order to succeed. You can't do this on your own. Moses's father-in-law, Jethro, points this out when he comes for a visit.

> *"Why sittest thou thyself alone, and all the people stand by thee from morning unto even?"* Exodus 18:14

Moses's reply was much the same as yours would be today. He says, *the people come unto me to inquire of God.* Jethro could see that Moses was overloaded and nearly burned out. There are many, many leaders who are burned out today for the exact same reason. Maybe you are there now. The load we shoulder can weigh us down causing anxiety, depression, and eventually burnout. Moses could not do it alone; it was too much for him.

Jethro says in verses 17-18,

> *"The thing thou doest is not good. Thou wilt surely wear away, both thou and this people that is with thee: for this thing is too heavy for thee; thou art not able to perform it thyself alone."* Exodus 18:17-18

Notice he mentions the people Moses is connected with. If you wear away, the people will too. When we as leaders become frustrated, it effects everyone around us.

Jethro recited the problem, but he also summoned the solution. He advised Moses to find able men and women to help him balance the load. You must have a support team of honest people who hate covetousness. The people who support you can't be jealous of your blessings. They need to be able to lighten your load and relieve stress, not add to your struggle. This is the team that you select. Remember, when you designate authority it will be easier for you, and your ministry will last.

"Two are better than one; because they have a good reward for their labor. For if they fall, the one will lift up his fellow: but woe to him that is alone when he falleth; for he hath not another to help him up. Again, if two lie together, then they have heat: but how can one be warm alone? And if one prevail against him, two shall withstand him; and a threefold cord is not quickly broken." Ecclesiastes 4:9-12

Moses was reminded many times that he could not do this alone. One of the primary reasons that we see burned out ministers today is that they try to do everything themselves. Many have become wearied in well-doing and are ready to walk away. If you try to fix everything, do everything, and carry everything yourself, you are setting yourself up for failure. We are not designed to do that. I encourage you as you seek the Lord to know that help is on the way!

The Art of Delegating Authority

Through Jethro, God told Moses to appoint leaders to serve as judges for the people, but to deal with the significant issues himself. As a leader, you stand in authority. But it is important to know when and how much authority to give to your team. Knowing your people is key. Do not be too hasty in trusting people with authority. Test them with a little first, and allow them to prove themselves and grow.

We see in Numbers how God directed Moses to start giving some of his authority to Joshua. He said,

> *"Put some of your honor and authority upon him, that all the congregation of the Israelites may obey him."*
> Numbers 27:20, AMP

Even God acknowledged that Moses held authority, but at the appropriate time, commanded him to share his load with Joshua. Leaders of the church should be rulers, not dictators. Once your people have come alongside you and demonstrated their faithfulness, you should begin to closely observe their talents. Take stock of their gifts and make use of them for the glory of God.

When God directed Moses to build the tabernacle, Moses sent Bezaleel to provide him with the knowledge and experience needed to construct an elaborate edifice.

We see this provision again when God put it in David's heart to establish a musical ministry in the Temple in Jerusalem. God sent Asaph, Jeduthem, Hernan, and a host of singers, songwriters, and musicians to ensure that David had the right tools to fulfill his vision.

If God is the architect behind your vision, he will place people in your life to help bring that vision to pass. God will provide all you need, but you have to be willing to put your trust in your team. Don't be afraid to give them some of the work, responsibility, and power. God will send you people who have the ability to pray, give, and work. Allow them to make decisions. There is no way you can oversee every detail of every operation. It will destroy you.

Part of your job as a leader is to discern and scope out those whom God has sent to assist you. Evaluate those working alongside you; become familiar with their strengths and weaknesses. As you get to know their character, you can gradually bring them into your inner circle. Over time you can test them by increasing their responsibilities. If they successfully complete their assignments, you can give them more authority and evaluate them in the eyes of the people. We see in Numbers Chapter 27 where Moses begins this process with Joshua.

> *"And the Lord said unto Moses, 'Take thee Joshua the son of Nun, a man in whom is the spirit, and lay thine hand upon him;' And Moses did as the Lord commanded him: and he took Joshua, and set him before Eleazar the priest, and before all the congregation: And he laid his hands upon him and commissioned him, as the Lord commanded through Moses."* Numbers 27:18, 22-23, AMP

God ordered Moses to give Joshua part of his authority so Israel would obey him. As a leader you cannot be intimidated by those who follow you. You are all part of the same team. Be careful not to measure your position in ministry against someone else's.

The Process of Delegation

The Bible lists three steps to delegating authority. First, God tells Moses to lay his hands on Joshua. Now at the time, the laying on of hands was an important and highly symbolic act. It was a public acknowledgement of one's connection to that person. But it was also an overt demonstration of authority and the receiver's submission.

Laying your hands on someone signifies the transference of power and authority. But be cautious, and seek God in this process. Do not lay hands on them if they do not share your vision. They must be of the same spirit, mindset, and attitude as you. If you ordain someone with a different spirit or vision, they will not submit to you; and it will be dangerous to promote them. Do not pick people who will poison your ministry and divide your flock. I have seen leaders who have promoted people in an effort to make them faithful, but that is out of order. My friend, you promote people *because* they are faithful.

In the second step, God told Moses to commission Joshua in the presence of all the people. The purpose of this was to show the people that the responsibility and authority had been transferred from Moses to Joshua. It's important to note that there is no authority without responsibility. We are dealing with a generation that longs for power, prestige, and promotion without the proper process. That's why many leaders are commissioning renegades and rebels instead of servants of the Lord. Above all else, this public display was to show the recognition Moses was giving Joshua and the delegation of authority. In other words, that which was done in private was now being made public.

Finally, God didn't want the transference of authority to be a mere act of symbolism. He wanted Moses to actually trust Joshua and give him some responsibility and power to rule. Trust is the difficult part. Moses trusted Joshua, and stepped back to make room for his new partner. Many leaders today are afraid to delegate authority because of greedy and power-hungry people. Some leaders have been burned by those they have promoted. They have given authority to the wrong people, and those same people have tried to take over the ministry by undermining their leader. Be cautious and seek God's council in this matter.

In conclusion, no man can build the Kingdom of God single-handedly. God anoints followers and puts in them all the tools and abilities *you* need to fulfill *your* vision. It's a partnership. Without followers, leaders are incapable of realizing their vision. Without leaders, there is no vision for followers to attach themselves to. When the vision is completed, no one person can claim the success. All the glory belongs to God for bringing in the right people at the right time to fulfill His plan. To God be all the glory, amen.

Chapter 3

STAFF INFECTION

Nothing hurts worse than the pain of betrayal. It breaks your heart, leaving a scar that only God can heal. In this decade of deception, betrayal surrounds us. It shows up in our family, our business, our ministry, among friends, and yes, even in our marriage.

I want to share with you now the story of Julius Caesar. Here was a man who brought Rome to the pinnacle of its majestic power, and was adored by the people. However, the Senate despised him. It wasn't long before a conspiracy was formed, and a plot to assassinate him began to take shape. The plan was for each of the Senators to stab Caesar so they would each share the blame.

On March 15, 44 BC, they made their move. They attacked Caesar like hungry lions, stabbing him repeatedly. History records that he fought fiercely against the attackers until he saw the face of Marcus Brutus, his closest friend, among the assassins. Caesar was known to be very fond of Brutus, and even treated him as a son.

Rumors say that Caesar's last words were, "Et tu, Brute?" meaning, "And you too, Brutus?" At which point he pulled his toga over his head, gave up fighting, and succumbed to his attackers. He lost his will to live the moment he saw Brutus. Betrayal killed Julius Caesar.

Nothing hurts as much as a wound from a friend. It can pierce your heart like an arrow. If you are working in leadership, it is only a matter of time before someone betrays you. It happened to Jesus, it happened to the Apostle Paul, and it will happen to you. Whether you are a boss at your workplace or the pastor of a church, it will happen. Perhaps it already has.

I've heard countless horror stories about friends turning on one another. I, myself, have experienced it on more than one occasion. I know how it leaves you feeling numb and more than a little shocked. You wonder how that person could betray you after all you have done for them. Often the person you've helped the most is the one who will try to destroy you. In the story I'm about to share with you, you will see betrayal at its finest.

In 2 Samuel 15 we find the house of David in chaos. David's son Absalom is plotting to overthrow him and take his throne. He went behind David's back and persuaded those closest to David to side with him. Verse 6 tells us that Absalom stole the hearts of the men of Israel. He won their loyalty by stroking their egos and undermining David's authority. Not only was his own son conspiring against him, but now his closest friends were as well.

As a leader, you have to be very careful who you allow into your inner circle. Some may seem charming, but in truth they are manipulating and conspiring behind your back. Be wary of those who would undermine your authority and sow discord among your leadership. Shut them down, and do it quickly.

Ahithophel was David's closest friend and counselor. In fact, David describes him in Psalm 41:9 as being, "Mine own familiar friend, in whom I trusted, which did eat of my bread." In Psalm 55:13 he calls Ahithophel "my guide and mine acquaintance." He goes on to say in verse 14 that they "took sweet counsel together, and walked unto the house of God in company."

Ahithophel was a wise man, and his advice was of great profit to David. But he wasn't just David's counselor; he was also his companion. David confided in him, sharing his dreams and future plans with him. Be careful whom you share your innermost thoughts with. You may discover later that the same person you trusted has betrayed that trust. They may even join forces with your greatest enemy in order to destroy you.

In verse 12 we see where Ahithophel betrayed David by joining Absalom. He went from being David's most trusted friend to his most formidable enemy. Consider this; without Ahithophel's help, Absalom's revolt would have never made it past its beginning stages. It always amazes me to see how our enemies will team up to take us out, even though they may hate one another.

Now Ahithophel had two goals in mind. The first was to make sure the separation between Absalom and David was beyond repair. We see in 2 Samuel 16:21 were he advises Absalom to go in to David's house and lay with his concubines in open defiance of his father.

Verse 22 says,

"So they spread Absalom a tent upon the top of the house; and Absalom went in unto his father's concubines in the sight of all Israel." 2 Samuel 16:22

Ahithophel wanted to be sure David knew what Absalom had done. That is why he advised him to do it in the sight of all Israel. He had to be sure the relationship between father and son was forever ruined. Today, there are people in the church who are masters of the divide. They know just what to say or do to help facilitate madness and keep the body of Christ divided. I believe there are many relationships today that could have been mended had someone not been there running interference and sowing discord. We are called to be peace makers, not peace breakers.

Ahithophel's next goal was to kill David. In fact, we see in the next chapter where he asks Absalom for permission to do just that.

"Moreover, Ahithophel said to Absalom, Let me choose twelve thousand men and I will set out and pursue David this night. I will come upon him while he is exhausted and weak, and cause him to panic; all the people with him will flee. Then I will strike down the king alone." 2 Samuel 17:1-2

Ahithophel pleaded with Absalom to let him take a band of soldiers to hunt down David and kill him. So now hatred burned in his heart for the man he once loved. But why? As it turns out, Ahithophel was the grandfather of Bathsheba. He was angry with David for his dealings with her and for having her husband murdered. All this time, offense had festered and grown in his heart. All it took to turn Ahithophel against David were a few sly words from Absalom's silver tongue. But the betrayal did not end with Ahithophel.

David's nephew, Amasa, was plotting with the enemy to take him out. He took a position as Captain of the Host in Absalom's army—an army that was formed for the sole purpose of overthrowing David. Nothing hurts worse than betrayal in your own family. It can tear your heart to shreds and leave you feeling hollow.

We go on to see in 2 Samuel 16 that as David fled from Absalom, he crossed through the lands of a man named Shimei. Shimei and David had been close friends since childhood. However, when Shimei saw David passing through, he threw rocks and dust at David and cursed him. I know there are situations where it seems like everyone and everything is against you, and you wonder whom you can trust. But sometimes you need to isolate yourself and walk alone; leave the room until the smoke clears.

Now I want to draw your attention to another form of betrayal. It's more subtle, though no less painful. We see in 2 Samuel where David is betrayed yet again by the man he had helped the most. David was in covenant with Jonathan, the son of Saul, and treasured his friendship. So when David learned of Jonathan's death, he inquired as to whether there were any decedents on which he might bestow kindness for Jonathan's sake.

That's when he learned of Mephibosheth, Jonathan's son who was lame. Immediately, he rescued Mephibosheth from Lo-debar and brought him to the palace where he ate at the kings table as one of the King's sons. In addition, he gave Mephibosheth all the lands that had once belonged to Saul. Yet, when David fled Jerusalem to escape Absalom, Mephibosheth did not join him: he abandon him. Even though he did not join with Absalom against David, he did not support David, either. Total abandonment is its own form of betrayal. When those you've helped the most walk out on you in your time of need, it can be crushing.

All of David's friends and staff turned against him and worked to undermine his leadership. Can you imagine your entire staff turning on you? Not just one or two, but all of them? Such was the case of David. He was being attacked on all sides and slaughtered by the enemy.

I have seen cases where disgruntled staff members have left a ministry to start their own church, causing a divide. And to make matters worse, they stole money from the ministry, unbeknownst to their leaders. Instead of repenting and asking for forgiveness, they tried to damage the church. These staff members would rather have destroyed the ministry than repaired it. Sometimes this happens when those under your leadership cannot take correction. Someone who will not submit to your authority may turn against you if disciplined. Be very careful when selecting your staff. Listen to the voice of God on this matter.

Absalom, Ahithophel, Amasa, Shimei, and even Mephibosheth betrayed David. Together they tried to orchestrate David's demise. He fled Jerusalem in fear, not knowing who he could trust. The very men who should have been supporting David and lifting him up were plotting against him.

Jesus too, had to deal with betrayal. Judas, his own disciple sold him out, sending him to his death. Pray and seek God when these situations arise. All the great leaders of the Bible dealt with issue and you will too.

My friend, that's when you stand still and trust God. When they're the one you share all your secrets with and the one you've call friend since your youth. When the entire support team comes against you all at a time, you have to trust God to protect you and pray for the wisdom of God on how to handle the situation.

There are many pastor's leaders who have exercised discipline concerning a staff member and trusted them, and they received it in love. But some have rejected and rebelled against leadership, and in some cases they walked out of that establishment and left that organization crippled or spiritually handicapped, or perhaps they tried to poison the people's mind against their leader.

Remember, hurting people always hurt people. And when the water is muddy, sheep want to drink; and they would drink from polluted streams.

So now David's entire staff is infected, and they are spewing out poison on everyone they come in contact with. But in spite of it all, David's experienced the protection of God, and he was thankful.

As a leader, you must hold it together when all others are falling apart. If there is someone sowing discord among staff workers, deal with them so it won't infect the other staff members.

Chapter 4

THE DANGER OF EXPOSURE

Today in this "tell all, speak all" society, nothing is private. This generation feels the need to express outward things that are felt inwardly. Yet they do not consider or perhaps even realize the damage this can cause. It has become a popular practice to speak publicly about issues that are best left private. At the end of the day, silence is golden. Don't misunderstand me, I do believe some things should be vocalized, but in the proper place and at the proper time.

I often wonder how many friendships, relationships, and marriages could have been saved had people not exposed their personal business or that of others. With so many advancements in technology today, people's problems are communicated in an instant. Social media has made it easy to publicize matters that are better dealt with behind closed doors. Be careful of exposing things that could be hurtful.

Let's take a look at Noah. Genesis 9 finds Noah in a drunken stupor, having consumed too much wine. The Bible says he lay naked and uncovered in his tent. Ham walked by and saw Noah's nakedness, but instead of covering him up as he should have, he went and told his brothers about it to further embarrass his father. However, Ham's brothers were wise enough not to join in. Instead, they took a sheet and entered his tent backward, so as not to see his nakedness, and they covered him. As a result, Ham was cursed while his brothers were blessed. There is great danger in exposing.

The Bible encourages us to restore instead of expose. You have to be careful not to further damage your brothers and sisters with your words or actions. Your motive should always be healing and restoration. Let's make a commitment now to cover our fellow Christians. Yes, correction is necessary, but we must always cover them.

"Brethren, if any person is overtaken in misconduct or sin of any sort, you who are spiritual [who are responsive to and controlled by the Spirit] should set him right and restore and reinstate him, without any sense of superiority and with all gentleness, keeping an attentive eye on yourself, lest you should be tempted also." Galatians 6:1, AMP

Remember that the area in which you judge someone else will be the same area that you yourself will be tempted and tested in. Leave the judging to God.

It's not wrong to confront someone, but it must be done out of love and a desire to heal. So many issues can be resolved in private if people will adhere to the counsel of the wise. Nathan confronted David concerning the murder of Uriah, Bathsheba's husband. As a result, David repented and was restored back to God.

I've known many great men and women of God who have been restored because their situation was handled in private. In each situation, they were very thankful and compassionate. On the other hand, I've witnessed situations in which a private matter was handled publicly. As a result, people have come against them, refusing to allow them to be restored to their rightful place in God.

I wonder how many ministries would still be in operation had their situation been dealt with properly. We are human, and as such we will make mistakes. It is important to remember that we all have a treasure within us. All too often we focus on the earthen vessel and lose sight of that treasure.

In Luke 15, Jesus gives the parable of the prodigal son who wasted his inheritance on riotous living, openly making a fool of himself. However, when he hit rock bottom, he came to himself. The son realized that he had not only embarrassed himself, but his family as well; and for that he was sorry. He messed up and fessed up. But more importantly, he got up, and went back home where he should have been all along.

Now here is something really significant. Consider the attitude of the father. He was open and receptive, awaiting his son's arrival with joy. Not one time did he remind the son of his faults or failures. Instead, he rejoiced saying, "My son was lost, but now he's found!"

I've never seen a time where there is so much jealousy and strife among leaders as there is now. We are called to encourage, strengthen, and cover our fellow Christians in prayer. There is such a spirit of competition nowadays, and it is destroying ministries.

When David learned of Saul's death he commanded that the people *"Tell it not in Gath, publish it not in the streets of Askelon: lest the daughters of the Philistines re-*

joice. " 2 Samuel 1:20 He didn't want news of Saul's death to reach Gath, because it was enemy territory. Exposing your brothers and sisters will only give the enemy cause to rejoice.

I remember fifteen years ago a family visited me at my home. They told me they were going to expose a preacher who had done some terrible things to their family, and asked for my wisdom on the matter. I asked them to prayerfully consider their action, and try forgiving instead. We were then able to arrange a meeting in which he apologized, and in return the family apologized to him. It brought restoration to the situation. We were able to correct the wrongs and cover both the preacher and the family.

James 5:16 says, *"Confess your faults one to another, and pray one for another, that ye may be healed. The effectual fervent prayer of a righteous man availeth much."* Let's start a healing campaign where we can build a safe refuge for our brothers and sisters who have been battle worn and battle torn. Give them help and counsel. They need to be fully restored back to God. Stop lynching our leadership and start healing. Ask yourself, "Am I part of the problem, or part of the solution?" Remember, mercy given, mercy received.

Chapter 5

VENGEANCE IS MINE

In the preceding chapters we've discussed the importance of forgiving those who have tried to hurt you, either by destroying your character or undermining your authority. In this chapter I want to remind you that vengeance belongs to God. He is the final judge, and nothing gets by Him.

"Say not thou I will recompense evil, but wait on the Lord, and he shall save thee." Proverbs 20:22

It's so tempting to take matters into our own hands. In fact, it's in our very nature to settle issues ourselves. However, it's not our place. This is a test that we all often fail. Trying to take care of it yourself will only make matters worse. Wait for the Lord. He will avenge you.

In Deuteronomy 32:35 God says,

"To me belongeth vengeance, and recompense; their foot shall slide in due time: for the day of their calamity is at hand, and the things that shall come upon them make haste."

You have to trust God to vindicate you. He doesn't need your assistance, just your obedience. God knows your hurts, sorrows, and suffering. Nothing can be hidden from Him. Nothing escapes His wrath. He sees every scheme, ulterior motive, and plot against you. His justice will always prevail. Don't take vengeance into your own hands; leave it in His.

They say hurting people hurt other people, and it's true. There are so many wounded people out there seeking revenge. Maybe someone has hurt you, and you feel a need to settle the score and make them feel the same way, but this is where you have to trust God. He knows how to handle it. If you try to do it yourself, it will only bring more pain.

Perhaps the biggest challenge in this area is timing. When will God avenge you? The Bible tells us that God is slow to anger, and everything is done in his time. Even when you feel like God has forgotten, remember His timing is perfect. Be patient. When the time is right, He will judge the matter. He is fully aware of your situation. Relax and give it to God. Nothing gets by Him. Even if a judge rules against you in a court of law, there is a higher judge that will rule in your favor. However, it is difficult to be patient and wait on his verdict. You think that if you do something about it, it will bring resolve in your spirit. Or if you say something, at least you're getting it off your chest. But no, vengeance belongs to God. Give it up to Him.

Let me turn your attention to the story of Naboth's vineyard. King Ahab desired Naboth's vineyard, which joined his own property. The Bible shows us where Ahab made Naboth an offer.

> *"And Ahab spake to Naboth, saying, Give me thy vineyard, that I may have it for a garden of herbs, be-*

cause it is near unto my house: and I will give thee for it a better vineyard than it; or, if it seem good to thee, I will give thee the worth of it in money. And Naboth said to Ahab, The Lord forbid it me, that I should give the inheritance of my fathers unto thee." 1 Kings 21:2-3

It is important to note here Naboth's unwillingness to part with his inheritance. Even though Ahab made him a good offer, Naboth would not take it. Never sell your spiritual inheritance, no matter what the enemy offers you.

The Bible tells us that Ahab went home angry and sullen because Naboth would not part with his vineyard. He laid in his bed sulking, and refused to eat. When his wife, Jezebel, discovered the reason for the king's behavior, she told him not to worry; she would get the vineyard for him. Notice, anything obtained outside the will of God will only come back to haunt you. If it isn't God given, release it and let it go. It will not prosper.

In verse 8, Jezebel plots against Naboth. *"She wrote letters in Ahab's name, and sealed them with his seal…"* In these letters, she persuaded men to speak against Naboth, saying that he cursed God and the King. As a result, Naboth was taken outside the city and stoned to death even though he was totally innocent.

As soon as King Ahab heard of Naboth's death, he left immediately to go take possession of his vineyard. Now, at this point in the story it looks as though Ahab has gotten away with his crime. He got the vineyard he wanted, and didn't have to pay anything for it. However, what is done in the dark will always come to light.

"Dearly beloved, avenge not yourselves, but rather give place unto wrath: for it is written, Vengeance is mine; I will repay, saith the Lord." Romans 12:19

Often, it seems as though the wicked go unpunished. Let me remind you, God will bring a day of reckoning. You can trust God to handle your situation. He is fully aware of your circumstances, and every plot, ploy, and plan of your enemies. Nothing gets Him. God will bring justice to your situation.

"And the word of the Lord came to Elijah the Tishbite, saying, Arise, go down to meet Ahab king of Israel, which is in Samaria: behold, he is in the vineyard of Naboth, whither he is gone down to possess it. And thou shalt speak unto him, saying, Thus saith the Lord, Hast thou killed, and also taken possession? And thou shalt speak unto him, saying, Thus saith the Lord, In the place where the dogs licked the blood of Naboth shall dogs lick thy blood, even thine." 1 Kings 21:17-19

Here we see the vengeance of God in action. Ahab thought he had literally gotten away with murder. He was enjoying the land he had wrongfully possessed, that is, until God showed up. God spoke to Elijah, and sent him to pronounce judgment over Ahab. Not only did the prophet recount Ahab's crimes, but he also foretold of Ahab's death. Elijah prophesied that Ahab would die in the same place that Naboth was killed, and the dogs would lick up his blood. So don't worry about what your enemy is up to; reckoning day is coming.

We see 2 Timothy 4:14 where Paul says,
"Alexander the coppersmith did me much evil, but the Lord reward him according to his works."

Paul was hurt by Alexander; Joseph was sold by his own family; Jesus was betrayed by Judas; and the list goes on and on. If you've been in ministry for any length of time, someone has probably tried to harm you; it comes with the territory. But you have to let God settle it for you. For me, this has been the hardest lesson to learn.

People are always looking for someone to blame, and often that blame is cast upon their leaders. It's difficult to operate in a position of leadership when people blame you, lie about you, falsely accuse you, and turn against you. You cover their mistake, and they crucify you. It leaves you feeling defenseless. But God says to leave them alone, and let Him avenge you.

"Vengeance is mine, I will repay." Romans 12:19
"But if ye forgive not men their trespasses, neither will your Father forgive you your trespasses." Matthew 6:15

Jesus warns that an unforgiving heart will destroy you in the end. Even when He was being crucified by the very people He was trying to help, He asked the Father to forgive them.

In fact, in Romans 12:20-21 Paul directs you to feed your enemy if they are hungry and if they are thirsty to give them something to drink. In doing so we *"heap coals of fire on his head."* Romans 12:20 In verse 21 he says, *"Be not overcome of evil, but overcome evil with good."*

Let's take a moment to look at the psychology of these verses. You know that God is going to take up your cause and see that justice is done. So now you're free from the burden of revenge. You no longer have to carry your anger, bitterness, and resentment. Let it go, and let God take care of it.

Chapter 6

THE DANGER OF COMPARING

Comparison springs from insecurity, and it can only have one of two outcomes. Either it will produce pride or a feeling of inferiority. Both can be deadly to a ministry. There are so many people in the body of Christ today that are living a competitive lifestyle—always battling to prove themselves superior. I'm here to tell you, God didn't call you to be like someone else. He called you to be you. So stop worrying about what someone else is doing and be the best YOU, you can be.

"For we dare not make ourselves of the number, or compare ourselves with some that commend themselves: but they measuring themselves by themselves, and comparing themselves among themselves, are not wise. But we will not boast of things without our measure, but according to the measure of the rule which God hath distributed to us, a measure to reach even unto you." 2 Corinthians 10:12-13

The Apostle Paul was careful to avoid comparing himself with others. In fact, he criticized teachers who sought to highlight their own goodness by comparing themselves with others rather than with God. Comparing your ministry with another's can cause pride to rise up in you, and a sense of superiority to poison your mind. Conversely, it can leave you feeling downhearted and insignificant. But when we measure ourselves against God's standards, it becomes obvious that none of us are good enough. Romans 3:23 states that we *"all have sinned, and come short of the glory of God."*

Be careful not to envy someone else's success, or their material goods. Stop comparing the size of your congregations, and the level of your teachers, preachers, or singers. If you see someone walking in favor, compliment and encourage them instead of fighting against them. You can't be them any more than they can be you.

Charles Swindoll once said, "Rabbits don't fly, eagles don't swim, squirrels don't have feathers, and a duck would look funny climbing a tree. Stop comparing and enjoy being you. There's plenty of room in the forest."

God will never judge you based on someone else's calling. And if He doesn't do it, why should you? There is not another person just like you anywhere in the world. You don't have to mimic someone else's ministry. God gave you your own assignment, gifting, anointing, and vision. How you perform it is up to you.

There are many different ways to cook a chicken: baked chicken, fried chicken, barbequed chicken, chicken casserole, and chicken on a stick, to name a few. But at the end of the day, it's all still chicken. Paul puts it this way in 1 Corinthians 12:20, *"But now are they many members, yet but one body."*

In 1 Corinthians, we find the saints divided. There is contention regarding leadership in the church. One group would say, I am of Paul, another, I am of Apollos, or I am of Cephas, and still another, I am of Christ. Paul rebuked them saying,

> *"Is Christ divided?"* 1 Corinthians 1:13
> *"Who then is Paul, and who is Apollos, but ministers by whom ye believed, even as the Lord gave to every man. I have planted, Apollos watered, but God gave the increase."* 1 Corinthians 3:5-6

Don't live the rest of your life in jealousy and hatred toward others. Stop disrespecting, belittling, and competing against your fellow Christians. We are supposed to edify and build up one another. Galatians 6:2 says to *"bear ye one another's burdens, and so fulfil the law of Christ."* We are called to help and heal our brothers and sisters, not hurt and tear them down.

> *"Then Peter, turning about, seeth the disciple whom Jesus loved following; which also leaned on his breast at supper, and said, Lord, which is he that betrayeth thee? Peter seeing him saith to Jesus, Lord, and what shall this man do?"* John 21:20-21

Even the disciples fell into this trap. Peter was too concerned about how John's ministry would compare to his own. We see further down in verse 22 where Jesus rebukes him saying, *"What is that to thee? Follow thou me."*

Too many people today are focused on other's gifts, visions, dreams, accomplishments, and favor. Instead, we should be focusing on maximizing our own gifting for the glory of God. Praise God for the talent and gift He has given you. Learn to be yourself. Speak from your heart, the way you would say it. Do the work God has called you to, and do it how you would do it, not the way someone else would. Don't live in misery and insecurity. Know your anointing and gifting, operate in your calling, and be secure in who you are. If you develop a competitive, comparative attitude, it will only hurt you.

Perhaps it's time to do a self-check. Is it difficult for you to support others? Encourage them? Pray for them? Rejoice when they are promoted? Are you intimidated by the giftings of others? Are you jealous when others receive more praise than you? If you answered yes to any of these, you have engaged in comparing. Beware. This is a dangerous trap.

Saul killed a thousand men in battle, but David killed ten thousand. The Bible tells us how Saul was jealous of David and wanted to destroy him. Both men had an amazing victory, but because David was praised more, it created a divide. Don't try to measure up with someone else's gifts, abilities, experiences, or expectations. Stop comparing yourself with others.

We are designed to grow together and flow together. We should build up our fellow Christians and esteem our brothers and sisters higher than ourselves. Each member of the body of Christ compliments the next. As parts of the same body, we are made to work with each other, not against. Remember, teamwork makes the dream work.

Chapter 7

HUMILITY VS. PRIDE

On three occasions in the New Testament we are told to be humble. In all of these instances, it comes straight from the mouth of Jesus. This law isn't just for leaders, but everyone in the church. Humility is a powerful tool; without it you cannot learn and grow.

The opposite of humility is pride. The definition of pride is, "a high opinion of one's own importance." How can you learn if you think yourself more important than those around you? This spirit breeds competitiveness in the body of Christ. People influenced by pride are always seeking acknowledgement of their superiority, but are never satisfied. Be cautious, as this is a formidable instrument of the enemy.

"Pride goeth before destruction, and a haughty spirit before a fall." Proverbs 16:18

As I have mentioned in previous chapters, pride is deadly spirit, nearly undetectable to those in its grasp. People will judge immorality or murder but will tolerate pride or disregard it altogether. Why? Because it is an issue of the heart. It's colorless, odorless, and tasteless. Often others will see it in you while you yourself are blind to it. It's like having bad breath—everyone can smell it, except you.

The Bible warns against the lust of the flesh, the lust of the eyes, and the pride of life. Yet eighty percent of our preaching today only focuses on the first two. Why? Because those are sins that we can see with our natural eyes. Pride is far more subtle. It is an inner issue.

From where does this spirit originate? Let's examine the Word of God. The first sin ever committed wasn't fornication, adultery, drunkenness, or murder. It was pride. It happened first in heaven, committed by an angel named Lucifer. Lucifer's pride led to a rebellion in which he and a third of the angels turned against the Creator. Pride will always lead to rebellion. It is an outer manifestation of an inner issue.

Ezekiel 28 outlines Lucifer's downfall. Verse 12 describes him as being *"full of wisdom, and perfect in beauty."* He was proud of his own wisdom and beauty, even though they were gifts imparted to him by God.

> *"Thou was perfect in thy ways from the day that thou wast created, till iniquity was found in thee. By the multitude of thy merchandise they have filled the midst of thee with violence, and thou hast sinned: therefore I will cast thee as profane out of the mountain of God: and I will destroy thee, O covering cherub, from the midst of the stones of fire. Thine heart was lifted up because of thy beauty, thou hast corrupted they wisdom by reason of thy brightness: I will cast thee to the ground, I will lay thee before kings, that they may behold thee."* Ezekiel 28:15-17

Verse 15 says that Lucifer was perfect until iniquity was found in him. Verse 16 says the multitude of merchandise had filled him with violence. In other words, it is an inner issue. Finally, we get to the root of the problem in verse 17. It says his heart was lifted up because of his own beauty.

We observe this often in the church today. People seek to lift themselves up because of their own knowledge, money, or position. Satan was cast down because of pride, and those who give into pride will be cast down as well.

> *"How art thou fallen from heaven, O Lucifer, Son of the morning! How are thou cut down to the ground, which didst weaken the nations! For thou hast said in thine heart, I will ascend into heaven, I will exalt my throne above the stars of God: I will sit also upon the mount of the congregation, in the sides of the north: I will ascend above the heights of the clouds: I will be like the most High. Yet thou salt be brought down to hell, to the sides of the pit."* Isaiah 14:12-15

What caused Lucifer to rebel? Pride. His problem here lies in two words—**I** and **will**. I will exalt my throne above the stars of God. I will sit on the Mount of the Congregation. I will ascend above the heights of the clouds. I will be like the Most High.

Satan believed he was equal to God, but God has no equal. Pride led to the sin of equalization. You can never receive from a person if you believe you are of equal status. You must humble yourself and submit to your leaders. Matthew 23:12 tells us, *"Whosoever exalts himself shall be brought low, and whoever humbles himself shall be raised to honor."* AMP

Humility is key. The Bible is replete with examples of its importance. Remember, we were not created to be higher than God. Man was created from the dust of the earth, not the clouds above.

Chapter 8

THE SPIRIT OF GEHAZI

I want to share with you the story of Gehazi, Elisha's servant. Now Gehazi was a faithful servant, and of great assistance to Elisha. Thank God for those armor bearers who are faithful to their leaders! However, we see in 2 Kings 5 where Gehazi's weakness became his downfall.

Verse 1 tells us of Naaman, a captain of the host of the king of Syria and a mighty man in valor. The Bible says he was afflicted with leprosy, so his king sent him to Israel to be healed. Not only that, but that he gave him ten talents of silver, six thousand pieces of gold, and ten changes of raiment to pay for his healing.

In verse 9 we see where Naaman shows up at Elisha's door, asking to be healed. Elisha sends him to wash in the Jordan seven times. Naaman does as Elisha says and "his flesh came again like unto the flesh of a little child, and he was clean." So Naaman returned to Elisha to thank him and to pay him the money sent by his king.

"Elisha said, 'As the Lord lives, before Whom I stand, I will accept none.' He urged him to take it, but Elisha refused." 2 Kings 5:16, AMP

Elisha refused payment for the miracle for two reasons. First, he knew that God had performed the miracle, not him. He was only the instrument that God had used. It's important we remember that today. God uses us to bring deliverance, healing, and breakthroughs in the lives of many. But give God all the glory.

Secondly, Elisha didn't want to be associated with the sorcerers of the day who sold their gifts and charms for material gain. However, Gehazi thought Elisha was missing an opportunity. After all, Naaman was a foreign leader from a wealthy state. So he had plenty of resources. In fact, in verse 20 Gehazi says, "Behold, my master has spared Naaman this Syrian, in not receiving at his hands that which he brought."

Gehazi was ruined by his familiarity with sacred things. At one time he was obedient, faithful, and loyal. He was impressed and was moved in his heart by the signs and wonders he saw. Gehazi had followed Elisha with pure motives, and no hidden agendas. Day after day he witnessed miracles, and saw the power of God flow through Elisha. But little by little the supernatural became common place, and the extraordinary became ordinary. Because he took these miracles for granted, he now saw them as a means for profit instead of as gifts from God.

Later on in verse 20, Gehazi takes it upon himself to accept payment from Naaman. He says, "I will run after him, and take somewhat of him." So now greed has seeped into Gehazi's heart.

Be careful who you trust to represent your ministry. Those around you may be operating under the influence of a spirit. Gehazi had a spirit of greed that drove him to seek personal gain.

> *"So Gehazi followed after Naaman, And when Naaman saw him running after him, he lighted down from the chariot to meet him, and said, Is all well? And he said, All is well. My master hath sent me, saying, Behold, even now there be come to me from mount Ephraim two young men of the sons of the prophets: give them, I pray thee, a talent of silver, and two changes of garments."* 2 Kings 5:21-22

Not only did Gehazi go behind Elisha's back, but he also lied about him and misrepresented him to Naaman. So Naaman, being grateful for his healing, told Gehazi to take double what he asked for.

Meanwhile, Elisha realized Gehazi was missing. Gehazi should have been by Elisha's side, guarding God's anointed one, but he wasn't there. Elisha sent for him to ask him where he'd been.

> *"He went in, and stood before his master. Elisha said, 'Where have you been, Gehazi?' He said, 'Your servant went nowhere.'"* 2 Kings 5:25, AMP

Now Gehazi lied to Elisha's face, not just behind his back. But God gave Elisha discernment in the matter. He says in verse 26,

> *"Did not my spirit go with you when the man turned from his chariot to meet you?"* 2 Kings 5:26, AMP

There stood Gehazi, who had been a good and faithful servant, condemned for covetousness. As a result of his greed, he was cursed with the same leprosy that Naaman had been healed of. Gehazi had been so privileged, working side by side with Elisha and witnessing God's power, but it did not save him from his weakness.

As a leader, you must ask God for discernment concerning those you place in positions of leadership. You don't want a Gehazi slipping in among your ranks.

Chapter 9

THE SPIRIT OF KORAH

Numbers Chapter 16 outlines the story of Korah, a man who incited a rebellion against Moses and Aaron. Korah had become jealous of the positions Moses and Aaron held, so he—along with two hundred and fifty chief princes—went to confront them.

> *"And they gathered themselves together against Moses and against Aaron, and said unto them, Ye take too much upon you, seeing all the congregation are holy, every one of them, and the Lord is among them: wherefore then lift ye up yourselves above the congregation of the Lord?"* Numbers 16:3

They went a step further and accused Moses and Aaron of taking them out of Egypt—which they believed was the real 'land flowing with milk and honey'—to let them die in the wilderness. These men claimed that Moses had made himself prince over the people and blinded them to the fact that he had not produced what was promised. Where was this Promised Land, this inheritance of the fields and vineyards?

Every accusation Korah and his followers brought against their leaders exposed their own motives. The Bible says in Romans 2:1, *"For wherein thou judgest another, thou condemnest thyself; for thou that judgest doest the same things."*

We observe the spirit of Korah operating in the twenty-first century. It is alive and well in our churches. This spirit will always challenge your leadership. Let's put this story in a modern context. It's the same accusations you, as a leader, have dealt with or will be dealing with. There are people in the church who would say that you have too much authority, because you're not the only one who hears from God. They will begin to say that you're leading the church in the wrong direction, or perhaps they will even accuse you of lying from the pulpit. In all of these instances the people are rebellious, and it is the spirit of Korah.

Let me clarify by saying that God does speak to different people in the church. However, he will not do it around or over the leaders in the church. He is a God of order, not disorder. Korah is a rebellious, prideful, independent, and anti-Christ spirit. It will challenge your authority as a leader, because it will not submit. No one can promote themselves or grant a position of spiritual authority. Promotion comes only from God.

If you are reading this now, and harbor rebellious feelings toward your leader, remember this—God has given your leader spiritual authority in the church. In order to come in line with God's plan, you must submit. They are God's mouthpiece. To rebel against your leader is to leave yourself unsupported, uncovered, and unprotected. Never leave your spiritual covering. It's their job to feed, protect, and correct their flock. It is an important and weighty task, for they keep watch over your soul. Don't be afraid of submission. Follow your leaders; they will lead you to greener pastures.

Do not allow yourself to become associated with Korah. It seeks people to attach itself to. But when judgment falls on the spirit of Korah, it also falls on those connected to it. The Bible says in verse 33, *"They and all that appertained to them, went down alive into the pit..."* Don't let Korah influence you. Wait for God to elevate you.

> *"Humble yourselves therefore under the mighty hand of God, that he may exalt you in due time."* 1 Peter 5:6

God instructs us to be humble. It is his job to decide when to elevate us. At the right time, he will lift you up regardless of other people's opinions. Psalm 75:7 tells us,

> *"But God is the Judge! He puts down one and lifts up another."* AMP

Korah committed the sin of equalization. He and his clan believed themselves equal to Moses. You can't receive from your leader if you think you're on the same spiritual level as they are. In order to learn, you must humble yourself. Miriam and Aaron made the same mistake when they said, *"Hath the Lord indeed spoken only by Moses? Hath He not spoken also by us? And the Lord heard it."* Numbers 12:2 Verse 9 says, *"And the anger of the Lord was kindled against them..."*

Korah sized up the congregation of Israelites and felt that they needed him. In his eyes, Moses and Aaron had become old and feeble. What better time to challenge them than when he thought them weak? The spirit of Korah will always second-guess the decision of their leader. It self-appoints and resents the success of others.

Remember, when you dishonor or disrespect the leader God has appointed, you are inviting judgment. It is not the job of the people in the pews to determine the status of those in the pulpit. If your leader is in error or operating outside the will of God, it is his place to discipline them. He appoints leaders, and he can remove them.

We see this in the story of Saul. Saul refused to obey God, so God ripped the kingdom out of his hands and gave it to David. It's also important to note David's treatment of Saul. Saul tried to kill David out of jealousy. However, when David had the opportunity to kill Saul and rid himself of the threat, he did not. Why? He remembered the Word of the Lord. Psalm 105:15 tells us, *"Touch not mine anointed, and do my prophets no harm."*

Even though Saul was out of the will of God, David respected his position and waited for God to deal with him. If David knew enough not to touch Saul in his backslidden state, you should be doubly careful when your leader *is* in the will of God. I believe that many of the curses on people's lives today are due to them rebelling, opposing, and speaking against their leaders.

I've seen countless cases of Korah coming against leaders in the church, and they never come alone. People under the influence of this spirit will always bring a crowd to back them up. They form cliques to separate the church, then take those who follow them across town to start their own church.

In honoring your leader, you are respecting God's choice. By the same token, if you dishonor those whom

God has chosen, you are also dishonoring God. Korah refused to acknowledge Moses's God-given authority. He felt as though he had just as much authority as Moses did. He pulled rank and was destroyed for it. He went from refusing to follow to being swallowed. This problem is still prevalent in the church today. People still speak out against their leaders, and as a result are swallowed up in pride, strife, and envy.

There are so many people under the influence of controlling spirits who think it is their responsibility to police the church. My friend, that is not the case. It's not your job as a follower to correct your leader.

The apostle Paul wrote in 1 Corinthians 11:1, *"Be ye followers of me, even as I also am of Christ."* If you are in front of your leader, you are not following. Submission isn't your leader making you follow, but you asking them to lead. Remember, God put them in a position of authority for a reason. It's not to demean you, but to help you. Respect it.

Chapter 10

DISCERNING AND DISPELLING THE SPIRIT OF JEZEBEL

In order to understand the spirit of Jezebel, we must look at its biblical origin. Jezebel is first mentioned in the Bible as the rebellious and manipulative wife of King Ahab.

> *"And Ahab the son of Omri did evil in the sight of the Lord above all that were before him. And it came to pass, as if it had been a light thing for him to walk in the sins of Jeroboam the son of Nebat, that he took to wife Jezebel the daughter of Ethbaal king of the Zidonians, and went and served Baal, and worshiped him."* 1 Kings 16:30-31

Jezebel's influence caused about seven thousand prophets and countless other Hebrews to bow to Baal. She persuaded them to forsake the covenant, destroy the sacred alters, and kill the prophets who remained faithful to God. The influence of this spirit was almost single-handedly responsible for corrupting an entire nation. In modern times, Jezebel can claim the destruction of thousands of churches, marriages, ministries, and businesses. Beware of this lethal spirit. It is haughty, prideful, and hates submission. There is nothing good or encouraging about it. It opposes everything God wants to do. The spirit of Jezebel will parade around the church demanding attention and glorifying itself instead of God.

The name Jezebel literally means, "without co-habitation" or "un-husband." Jezebel was married, but she never submitted. The Jezebel spirit is fiercely independent and hungry for power and control. Its purpose is to discourage, frustrate, manipulate, and dominate leadership. A woman under the influence of a Jezebel spirit will publicly tear down her husband in order to gain dominance over him. This spirit will not allow itself to be on the same level as anyone else. It will only form relationships that it can dominate. Although this spirit sometimes appears to submit, it is only to gain some strategic advantage. In its heart, it will yield to no one.

Though Jezebel was a woman and is often referred to as such, this spirit is without gender. It can operate just as easily wearing a three-piece suit as it can a dress. Jezebel will target men and women with insecurities, jealousy, or a desire to dominate others. Those who are bitter from neglect or a misuse of authority are especially susceptible to this enemy.

Jezebel is a seductive spirit. Many believers have fallen prey to its persuasions. In her effort to gain control, Jezebel will employ any means of sexual perversion necessary. She uses sexual passions to draw and conquer those she would manipulate. The Bible says in 2 Kings Chapter 9 that when Jezebel heard that Jehu was coming she *painted her face.* Don't be distracted by Jezebel's outward appearance. Remember, she can hurt you without ever laying a hand on you. This is a deadly spirit.

Another mark of the Jezebel spirit is its hatred of prophets. Jezebel ordered the death of thousands of prophets, even though she claimed to be a prophetess herself.

"But I have this against you: that you tolerate the woman Jezebel, who calls herself a prophetess, and who is teaching and leading astray my servants and beguiling them into practicing sexual vice and eating food sacrificed to idols." Revelation 2:20, AMP

Don't misunderstand me; there are many women who are anointed of God. He calls women to minister and even to be prophetesses. But be wary. If someone claims to be a prophet, insists on recognition, and tries to undermine the leadership, you are dealing with the spirit of Jezebel.

Humility is a foreign concept to those being used by the Jezebel spirit. They will seek the spotlight. 1 Peter 5 says,

"Humble yourselves therefore under the mighty hand of God, that he may exalt you in due time."

God called us to be servants, not celebrities. Jesus taught, *"He that is the least among you all, the same shall be great."* Luke 9:48 Greatness is not measured by titles or college degrees, the car you drive or the clothes you wear, the size of your house or how big your church is. You greatness is measured by your humility.

Elijah vs. Jezebel

Don't be afraid when Jezebel shows up, because there is always an Elijah present to deal with it. Elijah is everything that Jezebel is not. He speaks the Word of God, while Jezebel operates in witchcraft and deceit. He is bold, but Jezebel is brazen. He is a true prophet; Jezebel is false.

Elijah is ruthless in righteousness, and Jezebel is vicious in evil.

We find in 1 Kings 18 where Elijah challenged 450 prophets of Baal and 400 prophets of Asherah to a show-down on Mount Carmel. The Bible tells us that these 850 false prophets and satanic priests ate at Jezebel's table. These were the most powerful, evil people that the kingdom of darkness could produce. Do not let yourself be persuaded to eat from her table.

The challenge was this:

> *"Let them therefore give us two bullocks; and let them choose one bullock for themselves, and cut it in pieces, and lay it on wood, and put no fire under: and I will dress the other bullock, and lay it on wood, and put no fire under. And call ye on the name of your gods, and I will call on the name of the Lord: and the God that answereth by fire, let him be God..."* 1 Kings 28:23-24

Six hours after the challenge began, the false prophets were still unable to produce fire. When twelve hours had passed,

> *"At noon Elijah began to mock them, saying, Cry aloud, for he is a god; either he is musing, or he has gone aside, or he is on a journey, or perhaps he is asleep and must be awakened."* 1 Kings 18:27

But Baal was only a graven image. He had ears, but could not hear; had a mouth but could not speak. They talked to their god, but he did not talk back.

"Who hath formed a god, or molten a graven image that is profitable for nothing?" Isaiah 44:10

Isaiah called them impotent gods that cannot produce, carved from stone and built by the hands of men. They had to pick Baal up and carry him.

I don't serve a God that I have to pick up and carry. My God picks up and carries *me*.

Finally, when evening came and Baal still had not shown up, it was Elijah's turn. He prepared his sacrifice according to the challenge, but he went a step further and had barrels of water poured over the bullock, the wood, and in the trench around it. Then he prayed. I wonder what would happen if our leaders would start to pray again? When Elijah prayed,

"Then the fire of the Lord fell and consumed the burnt sacrifice and the wood and the stones and the dust, and licked up the water that was in the trench. When all the people saw it, they fell on their faces and they said, 'The Lord, He is God! The Lord, He is God!'" 1 Kings 13:38-39, AMP

Elijah then ordered the prophets of Baal be captured and killed. Jezebel was enraged and threatened Elijah saying,

"So let the gods do to me, and more also, if I make not thy life as the life of one of them by tomorrow about this time." 1 Kings 19:2

Elijah was afraid and fled to the wilderness were he begged God to let him die.

Now ask yourself, how can Elijah run scared after God showed up and showed out on Mount Carmel? It's because Jezebel is a warring spirit that comes to distract you from your calling. Whatever you do, stay focused on God and don't abort your assignment.

Now in 2 Kings Chapter 9 we see Elisha, Elijah's successor, anointing Jehu as king and prophesying Jezebel's death at his hand. As Jehu approached Jezreel—the city where Jezebel was staying—he was met by two kings, Joram and Ahaziah.

> *"And it came to pass, when Joram saw Jehu, that he said, Is it peace, Jehu? And he answered, What peace, so long as the whoredoms of thy mother Jezebel and her witchcrafts are so many?"* 2 Kings 9:22

This should be a sign to us today. There can be no peace in your ministry as long as there is a Jezebel spirit in operation.

Jehu slew the two kings and rode on into Jezreel to confront Jezebel. This spirit must be confronted. Do not pet it, pamper it, or pacify it. Confront it, conquer it, and kill it. As leaders we must have the spiritual backbone to stand up to the forces of evil. Remember, God has given you authority over all the powers of the enemy. King Ahab was too weak and fearful to confront Jezebel. If you do not deal with this spirit, you will empower it. The world does not need one more leader backing down and resigning out of fear.

It took boldness for Nathan to confront David about killing Uriah. It took boldness for Isaiah to tell Hezekiah that he would die and not live. It took boldness for John to call the Pharisees and scribes a generation of vipers. And it will take boldness to confront this spirit because if you do not, it will infiltrate and destroy your church. But I decree this day, in the Name of Jesus, that no weapon formed against you shall prosper!

> *"And when Jehu was come to Jezreel, Jezebel heard of it; and she painted her face, and tired her head, and looked out at a window. And as Jehu entered in at the gate, she said, Had Zimri peace, who slew his master? And he lifted up his face to the window, and said, Who is on my side? Who? And there looked out to him two or three eunuchs. And he said, Throw her down. So they threw her down: and some of her blood was sprinkled on the wall, and on the horses: and he trode her under foot."* 2 Kings 9:30-33

Notice that Jehu was compassionate toward the eunuchs that were enslaved by her. He may have shown them mercy, but he would not compromise with Jezebel. Jehu's assignment was to take out the house of Ahab, and he wouldn't let anything distract him—not even her adornment. As a leader, you cannot be distracted by this spirit's outward appearance. Take this spirit out; it is deadly.

Finally, remember that the spirit of Jezebel has three other spirits associated with it: domination, manipulation, and intimidation. It will not submit to authority or take correction. It is a rebellious spirit that seeks power, position, and prominence. This spirit will raise hell wherever it goes. So be careful and ask God for discernment. Don't be blinded by what you see.

My prayer is this: *Lord, help me discern the spirit of Jezebel, every controlling spirit, every dominating spirit, every intimidating spirit, every manipulating spirit, every spirit of confusion, and every judgmental spirit. We cast it out in Jesus Name.*

Chapter 11

THE SPIRIT OF ABSALOM

I want to turn your attention now to Absalom, David's son. His story begins in 2 Samuel 13. Here we find Absalom enraged because his sister Tamar was raped by his half-brother Amnon. He was so angry, in fact, that he commanded his men to kill Amnon, after which he fled the country and went to live with his grandfather, Talmai, in Geshur.

Absalom remained in exile for three years, at which point Joab convinced King David to let Absalom return home. Here's an important lesson. Be wary of those who leave your ministry only to return later. They may carry bitterness back with them. We see this in the case of Absalom. He was bitter because he felt that David did not deal justly in the case of Tamar. So he allowed that bitterness to fester inside him and came up with his own solution.

In Chapter 15, Absalom was back in his rightful place, having been forgiven by his father. However, Absalom had not forgiven David; bitterness still lived in his heart. So the seed of rebellion was planted, which 1 Samuel 15:23 says is *"as the sin of witchcraft."*

The Bible tells us in verse 2 that he rose up early and stood beside the gateway, a place where all the men coming to and from the city passed. It's also important to note that he rode out to the gates each morning with chariots and horses, and fifty men to run before him. Why? Because it made him look important in the eyes of the people. Absalom talked with the people passing by, making them feel important and forming relationships with them. He listened to their problems and sympathized with them.

> *"And Absalom added, Oh, that I were judge in the land! Then every man with any suit or cause might come to me and I would do him justice! And whenever a man came near to do obeisance to him, he would put out his hand, take hold of him, and kiss him. Thus Absalom did to all Israel who came to the king for judgment. So Absalom stole the hearts of the men of Israel."* 2 Samuel 15:4-6

Here we see how this spirit operates. Absalom sat by the gate of the city looking for people who were discontented or dissatisfied. He would show them sympathy, saying, "If I were the leader, I would handle things differently." Beware the wound lickers. Those operating under the influence of this spirit will deliberately seek out people who have been hurt, especially by the church. Absalom's charming words act as a salve to people who have been wounded. Proverbs 31:30 tells us that charm and grace are deceptive. Charm can fool you. Be careful. A wolf can't infiltrate your flock if it looks like a wolf. No, it will come dressed as a sheep.

Why is this spirit so hard to deal with? Because people become emotionally attached to it because of the relationships it builds. This spirit appears to be nice and lovable. As a result, it is very popular. Absalom is a powerful spirit.

It is difficult to resist its charms. Love, kindness, and favor are its tools. Everyone likes to feel important and to be treated special. Who can resist that? Everyone loved Absalom, even David. But this supposed sweetness caused division. Absalom stole not only the hearts of people, but those of David's inner circle as well.

Unlike Korah and Jezebel, who are bold in their rebellion, Absalom is a very subtle spirit. But don't let it fool you. The spirit of Absalom will shipwreck any church. That's what makes this spirit so lethal; it's difficult to detect.

I want to share with you three signs that an Absalom spirit is at work in your church.

The first sign is disloyalty. Instead of standing strong with you—their leader—they will seek out certain kinds of people to align themselves with: the disgruntled, frustrated, discouraged, those with low self-esteem, baby Christians, in particular. They feed off gossip and complaints, so those bearing the spirit of offense are particularly easy prey.

Once they have built relationships with the people, they will go behind your back and begin to plant seeds of doubt concerning your leadership. This spirit will take a small matter and turn it into a major issue—anything to discredit their leaders. Those with an Absalom spirit will seem loyal and look like they're seeking to go to the next level, but they are selfish and cunning. Beware. They have a hidden agenda. Do not promote Absalom; disconnect from him, and pray for wisdom on how to deal with this conniving, destructive spirit.

Secondly, people with the spirit of Absalom will have a vision contrary to that of the leadership. Nothing you can do as a leader will satisfy those under the sway of Absalom because they have their own vision for the church. They will seek out other malcontents to support their vision. This spirit is cunning. It will tell the people exactly what they want to hear, saying, "I would take the church in this direction if I were in charge." It's so vital to the life of a church that the people come under the vision of the house. A contrary vision leads to division.

Finally, the spirit of Absalom will try to divide your church. It is a master of the divide, constantly causing dissension in the ranks, whispering and conspiring against leadership. Mark those who cause division. Don't befriend or promote them. The Lord hates those who sow discord among brethren.

> *"Now I beseech you, brethren, mark them which cause division and offenses contrary to the doctrine which ye have learned: and avoid them. For they that are such serve not our Lord Jesus Christ, but their own belly; and by good words and fair speeches deceive the hearts of the simple."* Romans 16:17-18

Absalom is a church-destroying spirit that is driven by cunning and a prideful need to feel legitimized. In an effort to gain support, they will often use Scripture to strengthen their argument. Individuals with the spirit of Absalom will seek out people who will agree with them, even if they are wrong. Eventually this will cause division and destruction.

The only way to deal with this spirit is to cut off all ties to it. Often, these people will leave the church out of rebellion, but want to stay in fellowship with those in the church. This is dangerous. It may sound good, but their motive is not fellowship. It's division. You have to confront this spirit. As a leader, you must speak the truth *in love*. Although sometimes hurtful, correction is always beneficial.

At all times, it is vital to the ministry for you to constantly and consistently guard the gate so this spirit doesn't gain a foothold in your congregation.

Absalom's story ended just like that of Jezebel and Korah. They fell from their positions because of pride, and their lives ended tragically and prematurely. Please be watchful. Give no place to the spirit of Absalom. It is headed down the path to destruction. Don't get caught up with it.

Chapter 12

CAUTION IN COVENANT

God is a covenant God. When we enter into covenant with Him, He is faithful and true to His Word. Likewise, when we enter into covenant with someone, He is faithful to honor that alliance. He is a sovereign God and will never violate the freedom of will or power of choice that He has given us. So be careful who you enter into covenant with, because it can drastically change your life, whether for good or bad.

You'll find many different examples of covenants in the Bible. Genesis 15:9-10 tells of God's covenant with Abram. This agreement was symbolized by sacrificing animals. In a powerful ceremony, the animals—with the exception of the birds—were split into halves that were then placed opposite one another. Next, the persons entering the agreement would walk between the pieces, symbolizing the two becoming one.

Another example is a covenant of salt. Salt was used for two reasons. First, it was a very rare commodity, because there was no salt in Israel. It had to be shipped in at great expense. So the giving of salt was symbolic of the value one placed in an alliance or friendship. Secondly, salt is a preservative, and therefore symbolic of the covenant lasting forever.

We see the power of the salt covenant at work in 2 Chronicles 13, when Jeroboam came against the house of David in war. He is warned against it in verse 5.

> *"Ought ye not to know that the Lord God of Israel gave the kingdom over Israel to David forever, even to him and to his sons by a covenant of salt?"* 2 Chronicles 13:5

But Jeroboam would not heed the warning, and instead led his men into battle. Because he came against the covenant of salt between God and David, 500,000 of his men were slaughtered. To this day, it remains the largest single-day slaughter in history. This is an excellent example of the seriousness of covenants.

> *"Again I say unto you, That if two of you shall agree on earth as touching any thing that they shall ask, it shall be done for them of my Father which is in heaven."* Matthew 18:19

A covenant denotes a binding agreement between two or more parties. When two people agree in authority in the earthly realm, God is bound to honor it, whether for good or bad. If you enter a covenant with someone whom you can come into agreement with, the result will be something powerful. Conversely, if you align yourself with the wrong people, you can become limited by their mindset. Because you are bound to them, their limitations become your limitations. You can only succeed to the degree of those you are aligned with. In principle, if you come into covenant with the wrong people, groups, friends, business partners, or spouses, you become unduly influenced by their beliefs and characteristics. Be careful, and seek the council of God before entering into a covenant.

Many marriages fail simply because someone has entered into covenant with the wrong person. Once you have entered the covenant of marriage, you may find out things you didn't know before. You think you are marrying your best friend, only to discover that he or she is your worst enemy. You quickly find out that there is another side to that individual, another face, another agenda.

In 2 Timothy 3, the Apostle Paul warns his son Timothy that in the last days men will be traitors, trucebreakers and lovers of their own selves. Never, in all my time as a minister, have I seen and experienced so many relationships turn sour as now. There is almost as much disloyalty in the ministry as among the brethren. I know of many churches, families, and businesses that have split because of a break in covenant. I grew up in a time when a man's word was his bond. When you agreed on something, you shook hands, and that sealed the deal. Nowadays, people sign contracts left and right with no intention of carrying out their obligations. That is not of God. He is a God of truth. It is so important to honor your words.

Do not enter into a covenant unless you first consult God. One of the best examples of the importance of this is found in Joshua, chapter nine. As the news of the Israelites' victories spread across the land, they were met with opposition, both directly and indirectly.

First, the kings of the region massed together to come against the Israelites. This was the direct attack, the one they could see coming and expected. But the second was far more subtle. We see in verse four where the Gibeonites, fearing for themselves, resorted to trickery. You can expect the same kind of opposition as you obey God's commands. Be cautious. The Gibeonites approached Joshua, pretending to be people from a far off nation that had come to aid Israel. The Bible tells us that *"Joshua made peace with them...and the princes of the congregation swore unto them."* Joshua 9:15

But here is their mistake. Verse 14 says that that the Israelites *"asked not counsel at the mouth of the Lord."*

Joshua and his leaders had the wisdom to consult God before leading their troops into battle, but when it came to the peace treaty, they made their own decision; they didn't inquire of God. That mistake cost them dearly. We must always acknowledge the Lord in all our ways. He will direct out path, especially in covenant.

In verse 16, the truth is finally revealed, and Joshua realizes that he has made a terrible mistake by unknowingly making an agreement with the enemy. However, the vow to protect the Gibeonites had already been made. The vow was not nullified by the Gibeonites' trickery. The Israelites still had to keep their word. Now Israel was aligned with the very people they had come to conquer. In Exodus 23:32, God had told them to make no covenant with them. So not only has Israel been tricked, but because of their carelessness, they are now in disobedience.

It is crucial to pray for God's will in these situations, especially when you're under pressure. That way, God can reveal their trickery before you join into covenant with them.

"Or if anyone unthinkingly swears he will do something, whether to do evil or good, whatever it may be that a man shall pronounce rashly taking an oath, then,

when he becomes aware of it, he shall be guilty in either of these." Leviticus 5:4, AMP

God takes vows very seriously, and commands that we keep them. This should encourage us to be cautious in pledging ourselves to others; it isn't something to be taken lightly. In my own life, I have learned this lesson the hard way. I have joined with people, believing them to be one thing, only to discover they were the opposite of what they portrayed. When their masks were removed and I could see what was hidden beneath, I was left in shock. This happens every day in ministry. You want to believe the best of people instead of thinking they might have a hidden agenda. We only see their calling instead of their character.

By failing to seek God's guidance and rushing ahead with their own plans, the Israelites were forced to deal with angry people and an awkward alliance. In order to be a successful leader, you have to be careful not to get over-confident in your own ability to make decisions. Though you may feel that you have all the facts and understand the situation, it is still wise to seek God's council before joining yourself to someone. This can keep a minor matter from becoming a major mistake.

Let's look at another biblical example of an unholy alliance. Deuteronomy 22:10 say that we should *"not plow with an ox and an ass together."* Here God is warning us against connecting with people who are incompatible with his plan for us. The ox and ass cannot work together because they have two different spirits, and it's counterproductive.

An ox is an animal with the attitude of a servant and a sacrificial nature. It is willing to work and submit to authority due to its teachable spirit.

On the other hand, an ass has a rebellious, stubborn, and contrary nature. It will constantly fight and work against everything you're trying to accomplish. That type of spirit will drain you and wear you out. Do not align yourself with people who have the same spirit as the ass. It is a dangerous arrangement, and will always end in hurt and heartache.

One spirit is good; the other is evil. One will submit; the other will rebel. One is a helper, the other a hindrance. One builds up, while the other tears down. Amos 3:3 says, *"Can two walk together, lest they be agreed?"* Remember, you will never have a head on collision if you are both moving in the same direction.

When you find yourself in covenant with people who are of a different spirit, it becomes a constant struggle for dominance. The Bible tells us in 2 Corinthians 6:14,

> *"Be ye not unequally yoked together with unbelievers: for what fellowship hath righteousness with unrighteousness? And what communion hath light with darkness?"*

All too often we find ourselves in this situation. We join covenant with people who end up working against us, whose nature is contrary to ours. They keep us from fulfilling God's plan and purpose in our lives. As a leader, you must pray for discernment in order to connect with the right spirit. Discernment means to perceive by intellect that which is unseen. Remember, not every good connection is a God connection. And if God isn't in it, you shouldn't be either.

Look at Solomon. He was the wisest man in all the world, yet because he connected with and convened with strange women, his heart was turned from God. Not only that, but he began to burn incense to idol gods.

My point is this, you will invariably take on the characteristics and attributes of whomever you are in covenant with. You share their ideas, problems, values, and beliefs. We are affected, whether for good or ill, by our connections. It is crucial to align yourself with God's plan for your life. I've witnessed so many cases were leaders have connected with the wrong people—people of a different spirit. They are in constant turmoil. If it doesn't fit, do not force it. Just release it and let it go.

Once you enter into covenant, you cannot go back on your agreement. God will forgive sins, but he doesn't cancel the consequences. Though he can bring good out of a bad situation, a covenant is still a covenant and must not be broken. It is vitally important to know and fully understand the environment and characteristics of anyone or anything that you are considering entering into a covenant with. Who you are connected with will shape and affect every area of your life.

Chapter 13

WISDOM IN CONFRONTATION

Confrontation is an integral part of ministry. The Bible tells us in Hebrews 12:6, *"For whom the Lord loveth He chastens..."* A time will come in the course of your ministry when you will have to confront someone. It cannot and should not be avoided. Confrontation is never easy and it may cause pain, but it is necessary. You have to address issues before they reach the boiling point and rage out of control. It's not going to go away unless you do something about it. As leaders, we hate confrontation and try to avoid it as long as possible. Our heart is for the people, and Satan tries to use that against us. However, if you don't confront an issue, it will only grow.

The Bible is a book of confrontations. Throughout the New Testament, Jesus confronts the Pharisees and Sadducees, calling them a generation of vipers. Joseph confronted his brothers. Elijah confronted Ahab, Jezebel, the prophets of Baal on Mount Carmel. Nathan confronted David about Bathsheba. Moses confronted Pharaoh, telling him to let God's people go. Just as these men of God had to confront problems, you, as a leader, must do the same. It's your duty to confront and correct. However, there is a proper process.

> *"Brethren, if any person is overtaken in misconduct or sin of any sort, you who are spiritual [who are responsive to and controlled by the Spirit] should set him right and restore and reinstate him, without any sense of superiority and with all gentleness, keeping an attentive eye on yourself, lest you should be tempted also."* Galatians 6:1, AMP

It's crucial to use wisdom in confrontation. If done properly, it can heal. If done improperly, it can be devastating. What is the best way to confront someone? First, pray about it. Pray for wisdom and discernment concerning the proper place, time, and manner in which you go about it. Even the right thing said at the wrong time can be disastrous.

Next, make sure you are approaching it with the proper attitude. You must confront with meekness, mercy, and love. Matthew 5:9 says, *"Blessed are the peacemakers: for they shall be called the children of God."* In order for confrontation to be effective, it has to come from a place of love, not from a desire to prove yourself right.

Never confront someone when you are angry. James 1:20 says it like this: *"For the wrath of man worketh not the righteousness of God."* If you confront someone simply to make yourself feel better, you are out of line. Anger will only elevate a situation rather than alleviate it.

Also, you would be wise to have a witness present. This prevents any false accusations from being spread by the person you are confronting. If you are alone when you confront someone, it will be your word against theirs, with no proof of the truth.

Lastly, you must be firm in confrontation. Do not leave them any wiggle room. If you are passive, they may simply shrug it off, and the problem will still be there.

Confrontation can be difficult, especially when it involves someone that people look up to. In the eyes of the people, this kind of person can do no wrong because they are master manipulators. It's scary to have to confront someone that you know everyone will feel sorry for. Nevertheless, it has to be done. As I said before, these problems won't go away on their own.

So my question is this; how much longer will you let the enemy frustrate you? How much longer will you tolerate and entertain these issues? If you let them continue to grow, they will be that much harder to rebuke. Be bold in righteousness and don't let these issues overtake you. In hindsight, you'll be glad you did.

Chapter 14

DEALING WITH ACCUSATIONS "HOW TO HAVE GRACE UNDER FIRE"

In ministry, you often have to deal with false accusations. We all are affected by it at some point. Circumstances will arise where you appear to be guilty, even though you are completely innocent. Sometimes people will make accusations against you *in public*, but will only apologize for their wrong *in private*, so you still appear guilty in the sight of others.

So, what do you do when this situation arises? How do you deal with it? Let's take a look at the Scriptures to find out.

Matthew 18:15 says,

"Moreover, if thy brother shall trespass against thee, go and tell him his fault between thee and him alone: if he shall hear thee, thou hast gained a brother."

Let's examine this Scripture. What do you think would happen if all Christians lived by this? It would certainly save a lot of pain. The Bible goes on to say in verses 16 and 17,

"But if he will not hear thee, then take with thee one or two more, that in the mouth of two or three witnesses every word may be established. And if he shall neglect to hear them, tell it unto the church: but if he neglect to hear the church, let him be unto thee as a heathen man and a publican."

It also is important to understand who your true enemy is. It's not the person telling the lies about you, but rather the satanic force that is driving them. Revelations 12:10 says that Satan is the accuser of the brethren. Anytime there are rumors, slander, and lies being tossed around, it's being hatched straight from the pits of Hell. You cannot reason with this spirit, so stop wasting your time chasing rumors. James 3:16 says, *"For where envying and strife is, there is confusion and every evil work."* Proverbs 6 tells us that God hates a false witness. An accusing spirit will try to sow contention and confusion. Beware, and don't fall into this trap.

Let's look again at the life of Joseph. Genesis 39 finds him in a sticky situation. Potiphar's wife was trying to seduce him and convince him to lie with her. When he refused, she continued to press him. Verse 10 says that she spoke with him day by day. Yet Joseph never gave into temptation.

Eventually Potiphar's wife became angry with him for his continued refusal. During their last confrontation, she grabbed hold of Joseph's garment, and in the process of getting away from her, he left his coat in her hands. She told her husband that Joseph tried to force himself on her. Because she had his garment, she had evidence to support her false accusations. Joseph was completely innocent, yet the evidence said otherwise. He was defenseless.

Have you ever tried to run from trouble only to find that you've actually run into trouble? My friend, we're living in a time where you don't have to actually be guilty to be considered guilty. All you have to be is accused. People will form opinions simply on hearsay. All it takes is one jealous person to make a false accusation. Maybe they are intimidated by you. Or perhaps they desire you, and are angry because you've rejected them. Such was the situation of Joseph. All the evidence was stacked against him. He was in a helpless situation where he could not defend himself. Joseph had no lawyer or even a friend he could talk to. He was alone. Not that Potiphar would have believed Joseph over his own wife anyway.

Have you ever found yourself in a similar situation? You feel helpless because there are no witnesses to back up your story? Many people believe that if they don't tell their story, someone will make one up to tell about them. Remember, you don't have to defend yourself. Trying to do so will only make the situation worse. This is particularly difficult, especially when your character is attacked. Potiphar's wife might have had Joseph's coat, but he kept his character.

Joseph was accused of forcing himself on Potiphar's wife, yet the Bible never mentions him trying to defend himself. Why? Sometimes, God will not allow us to speak on our own behalf, and we have to trust Him to vindicate us. You must be patient. God's judgment is sure. You don't have anything to prove to your friends, and your enemies won't believe you anyway. You just have to trust God to handle your circumstances.

Joseph did everything right in this situation. He showed his respect for Potiphar by not accepting his wife's invitation. Joseph considered both Potiphar's feelings and his trust. He mentioned in verse 8 the trust that Potiphar put in him by committing everything he had into Joseph's care. By refusing to lay with Potiphar's wife, he showed his respect for her.

Paul reminds us in Romans 13:14 to, *"Make not provision for the flesh, to fulfil the lusts thereof."* Again we see in 2 Timothy 2:22 where he tells his son to, "Flee also youthful lusts."

Don't meditate on the things that tempt you. Joseph ran from temptation, and you should, too. Remember, he never pursued Potiphar's wife, she pursued him. But his convictions were stronger than his fleshly desires.

And finally, he honored God. He says in verse 9, *"How then can I do this great wickedness, and sin against God?"*

Although Joseph did all things the right way and handled the situation correctly, he was still falsely accused. People don't have to have a reason not to like you; they still will tell lies about you and accuse you of things you did not do. Not only did Potiphar's wife tell her husband a lie about Joseph, but she also told all of the household staff and ruined Joseph's reputation. When people are angry and want revenge, they will do anything to discredit and destroy you.

What happens when you do everything right and still end up in prison? Consider this: if Joseph had spoken up and defended himself, his situation could have ended badly. And even though he was innocent, as a result of that situation he was a ruler of Egypt, second only to Pharaoh. Even though Joseph's situation seemed impossible, God stepped in and turned it around.

Maybe someone has been spreading lies about you, slandering your name, or perhaps they've even been unkind to you, but you have to forgive them. Let God fix it. God will get the glory in the end. Ride out the storm and outlive the lie. Don't quit and throw in the towel. Don't abandon your assignment. It will eventually work out for the best. Just like Joseph, you're being set up for something great. God always prepares you before He promotes you.

In previous chapters, I talked about the spirit of Korah opposing God's chosen leader, Moses. It ended with Korah and his followers being swallowed up by the earth. Speaking out against God's leadership will only set you up for failure. By your words, you sow the seeds of your own destruction. The Word of God clearly states in 1 Timothy 5:19, *"Against an elder receive not an accusation, but before two or three witnesses."* Remember the story of David. Saul was a jealous and controlling king, but David conducted himself wisely. Don't try destroy God's leader. If they are wrong, let God be the judge. By taking the matter into your own hands, you are putting yourself in the position of God, and you will lose His assistance.

I encourage you to pray for wisdom and peace in the face of accusations. Don't let the lies of the enemy affect your character. Stay true to the Word of God, and don't get involved in a war of words. God will be the judge. And his judgment is righteousness.

Chapter 15

PASSING ON THE MANTLE

I believe in the exceeding importance, especially in this day and age, of grooming the next generation of leaders. These future leaders are greatly suffering from a lack of mentorship. It is your responsibility as a leader to pour yourself into them. Prepare them to take your mantle when the time comes to pass it on. You need to invest your time, energy, and wisdom into creating a pattern for them to follow.

Through Eli, Samuel learned to hear and know the voice of God. John 10 tells us that, *"The sheep follow him: for they know his voice. And a stranger they will not follow..."* It's up to us to impart this knowledge to the younger generation. We are to guide them and teach them in the ways of God.

In previous chapters, I spoke on the transition of power from Moses to Joshua. Moses groomed Joshua for that position. Joshua worked side by side with him so that when the time came, he would be capable of taking over Moses's mantle. This was not just to prepare Joshua, but also to prepare the people to receive him. He had a great leader that he followed and submitted himself to. As a result, the old generation embraced the new in a beautiful transition.

Now we find Joshua in charge. He took up the mantle and picked up where Moses left off. Because Joshua now wore the mantle of Moses, the Lord tells him in Joshua 1:5, *"As I was with Moses, so I will be with thee: I will not fail thee, nor forsake thee."* God goes on to tell him in verse 6 to, *"Be strong and of a good courage."* Because Joshua was properly groomed and mentored, he was a great leader for his people. However, when it came time for Joshua to pass on the mantle, he had no one to succeed him.

Joshua died without passing the mantle to anyone else. Judges 2:10 tells us that after Joshua's death, *"There arose another generation after them, which knew not the Lord, nor yet the works which he had done for Israel."* Because he did not pass it on, his mantle died with him.

So often today, mantles fall to the ground without anyone to pick them up: mantles of healing, mantles of restoration, mantles of great visionaries, and many more. It's time that we, as the body of Christ, catch those mantles and embrace the calling that is on our life—much in the same way that Elisha caught Elijah's mantle.

First Elisha worked with and served under Elijah, walking with him and ministering to him. He was trained and mentored by Elijah so that when the time came, Elisha was able to pick up the mantle and continue on. However, like Joshua, Elisha did not pass his mantle on and it died with him. Don't let another leader leave here without having someone there to catch their mantle.

However, the next generation cannot catch a mantle unless it is first released. It is important for young leaders to connect with fathers of faith, so don't be afraid to mentor them. No leader will live forever. By refusing to step aside, you will hold back the next generation from fulfilling their purpose. A strong leader with integrity knows how to move themselves to the side, and make room for others. They know when they have contributed their share, and when it's time to hand over the reins. However, many in leadership are reluctant to give up the prestige, power, and financial benefits that their position provides, and therefore, guard it jealously.

Look at the relationship between Paul and his son, Timothy. Paul was not reluctant in his handing over the mantle to his son. Instead, he said,

> *"For I am now ready to be offered, and the time of my departure is at hand. I have fought a good fight, I have finished my course, I have kept the faith."* 2 Timothy 4:6-7

In saying that, he left a pattern for Timothy—and for us still today—to live by, as well as the tools he needed to be successful. Paul said, he fought a good fight. All of us have our own battles to fight. It is up to us whether or not they end well.

Next he said, he finished his course. "My course," not someone else's. God has a specific course set for your life. You may not finish first, second, or even third, but you will go down in history as a finisher.

And lastly, he says, he had kept the faith. Wow! What a proclamation. This pattern set by Paul guided Timothy as he continued on, bearing the mantle of his father.

How will you know when it's time to pass on your mantle? You must seek God's will and His timing. Sometimes though, it's difficult to give your blessing to a younger generation. Perhaps it's out of fear, insecurity, or intimidation. Whatever the reason, do not linger when

God has instructed you to hand over the reins to the next leader. So often those reins rest in failing hands because a leader refuses to release the mantle. When you refuse to pass on your position, the vision will vanish, the morale will be gone, and the church will be in a constant state of struggle.

My point is this: we must do our part to ensure that the next generation has the proper knowledge, tools, and training to be all that God has called them to be. Pray for wisdom and discernment in this area. And when the time comes, let go of the mantle and let it settle on someone else's life.

THE HISTORY OF MT. CALVARY POWERHOUSE CHURCH

Mt. Calvary was founded in February 1990, in Parma, Missouri, under the leadership of Dr. Ron Webb and Sister Georgia Webb, which was the beginning of their ministry in the Pastoral arena. Later, Dr. Webb combined Powerhouse Church and Calvary Baptist Church together as one body, which is now called Mt. Calvary Powerhouse Church, which remained in Parma for four years.

In 1995, the Church relocated to Malden, Missouri, where it prospered until moving to its current location at 1875 Speedway Drive in Poplar Bluff, Missouri.

For more information on the ministries of Dr. Ron Webb or Mt. Calvary Powerhouse Church, visit www.ronwebbministries.com.

ABOUT THE AUTHOR

Dr. Ron Webb is the pastor of the Mt. Calvary Powerhouse Church in Poplar Bluff, Missouri. Pastor Webb has been in the ministry for over 30 years. He attended Three Rivers Community College in Poplar Bluff, Missouri. He majored in Business Administration and was a former "Raider" basketball player. He earned a Bachelors of Theology from the International College of Bible Theology, and a Masters of Pastoral Studies in counseling, and a Doctorate in Theology from Midwest Theological Seminary. Dr. Webb also had the honors of doing the invocation at the inauguration for Governor Jay Nixon.

The unique ministry of Dr. Ron Webb is evident as he is anointed in the areas of church leadership and government. Dr. Webb has been considered by many to be "A Pastor To Pastors." His ministry is centered around "Restoration" and "Racial Reconciliation" and a sincere belief that we must "reach the lost at any cost." His preaching and teaching focuses on empowerment and hope.

Dr. Webb is the C.E.O. and President of the S.E.M.O. Christian Restoration Center, a center for individuals who might need a second chance on life. He is the founder and a lead instructor of "School of the Prophets Bible College" in Poplar Bluff, Missouri. The School of the Prophets offers the equipping needed to fulfill Jesus's command to "Go ye therefore, and teach all nations..." (Matthews 28:19) and the training and the experience to be a leader.

The Heartland Family Center, a homeless shelter for families, is the newest outreach ministry organized and founded in 2007 by Dr. Webb. The Heartland Family Center is owned and operated by the Mt. Calvary Powerhouse Church, it endeavors to serve those families whose circumstances have deprived them of adequate living and housing. In a Christ-like manner, families in need are provided housing and services to help them become self sufficient.

Covenant Ministries is another ministry that was designed by Dr. Webb to advance God's Kingdom by providing a fellowship in which men and women of God find mutual encouragement, edification, counsel, and participate in leadership and ministerial training.

Dr. Webb is married to Georgia Webb and they have three children, Ronnie Jr., Tony and Jackie (Webb) Brown, and two grandchildren, Jerrell Brown Jr. and Jaxson Brown.

NOTES

NOTES

NOTES

_____

_____

_____

_____

_____

_____

_____

_____

_____

_____

_____

_____

_____

_____

_____

_____

_____

_____

_____

_____

NOTES

Scriptural References

INDEX

B
Bakker, Jim 12
Brown, Jackie (Webb) 5, 103
Brown, Jaxson 5, 103
Brown, Jerrell Jr. 5, 103

C
Covenant Ministries 103

E
Edison, Thomas 13
Edmonson, Jasper 5

F
Ford, Henry 29

H
Heartland Family Center 103

J
Jackson, Sandra 5
Johnson, James A. 8

M
Malden, Missouri 101
Mt. Calvary Powerhouse
 Church 101, 102, 103

N
Nixon, Jay 102

P
Parma, Missouri 101
Poplar Bluff, Missouri 101,
 102, 103

R
Robertson, Benny 5

S
School of the Prophets Bible
 College 103
S.E.M.O. Christian Restora-
 tion Center 103
Sikes, Doug 5
Summers, Clinton 5
Summers, Clinton Jr. 5
Swindoll, Charles 53

W
Webb, Alfonse Jr. 5
Webb, Dave 5
Webb, Georgia 5, 101, 103
Webb, June Marie 5
Webb, Ron 4, 9, 15, 101, 102,
 103
Webb, Ronnie Jr. 5, 103
Webb, Tony 5, 103
Worley, Curtil 5

And we know that all things work together for good to them that love God, to them who are the called according to [his] purpose.

Romans 8:28